S0-CFT-885

presented to

from

A Christmas greeting from the heart.

Joy Notes at Christmas

Just for You, Grandchild

Illustrated by Beth Yarbrough

COUNTRYMAN

Project Editor—Terri Gibbs

Designed by Left Coast Design, Portland, Oregon

ISBN: 0-8499-9536-1

www.jcountryman.com

Printed in China

The trees
are ablaze
with
twinkling lights...

but you
give me
the most
delight!

These are some of
the things that
make you special...

_____

_____

_____

_____

_____

_____

You are
my joy
every day
of the year.

I hope this brings you cheer!

Little cheeks warm and red,
sweet, cheery dreams
while snuggled in bed...
of all that Christmas
brings.

Every good
and perfect gift
is from above.

James 1:17

You are...

God's gift to me!

A Christmas
prayer for you:

_____

_____

_____

_____

_____

_____

If I could give you any gift
in the world
I'd give you the gift of...

_____

_____

_____

_____

_____

_____

_____

Sing out merry tidings
Christmas time is here.
'Tis the season
of love
and laughter—
the jolliest time
of the year.

Along with you
love came into
my heart
to stay.

"Merry
Christmas
grandchild"
is the
cheeriest
greeting
of all!

CLAIRE EAMER

TRAITORS'
GATE

AND OTHER
DOORWAYS
TO THE PAST

Edited by Elizabeth McLean
Proofread by Tanya Trafford
Cover and interior design by Irvin Cheung / iCheung Design, inc.
Cover photos: (iron gate, Cape Coast Castle) © istockphoto/Benjamin Porter; (Traitors' Gate) © Jeff Hitchcock

We acknowledge the support of the Canada Council for the Arts, the Ontario Arts Council, and the Government of Canada through the Book Publishing Industry Development Program (BPIDP) for our publishing activities.

 ONTARIO ARTS COUNCIL
CONSEIL DES ARTS DE L'ONTARIO

Cataloguing in Publication
Eamer, Claire, 1947-
    Traitors' Gate : and other doorways to the past / by Claire Eamer.

Includes bibliographical references and index.
ISBN 978-1-55451-145-7 (bound).—ISBN 978-1-55451-144-0 (pbk.)

    1. Doorways—History—Juvenile literature. 2. World history—Miscellanea—Juvenile literature. I. Title.
NA3010.E24 2008   j909   C2008-901836-2

Printed and bound in China

Published in the U.S.A. by
Annick Press (U.S.) Ltd.

Distributed in Canada by
Firefly Books Ltd.
66 Leek Crescent
Richmond Hill, ON
L4B 1H1

Distributed in the U.S.A. by
Firefly Books (U.S.) Inc.
P.O. Box 1338
Ellicott Station
Buffalo, NY 14205

Visit our website at **www.annickpress.com**

For my parents, Arlene and Gib,
who introduced me to the wonder of history
in wood, brick, and stone

Contents

Traitors' Gate is a giant archway leading into the Tower of London. The Tower, a huge fortress that squats on the north bank of the River Thames, has served as royal palace, armory, prison, and many other things for more than nine centuries.

WHEN THE TIDE ROLLS UP the Thames from the sea, water floods the archway and small boats can sail through to a stone wharf within the Tower's outer walls. In the days when the river carried much of London's traffic, Traitors' Gate was a handy way to carry cargo and people to the Tower.

Sometimes the people who entered through Traitors' Gate were prisoners—important prisoners. During the 16th and early 17th centuries, state prisoners were often brought by boat to Traitors' Gate, led up the stone steps of the wharf, and locked in the Tower. Many died there, some by the executioner's ax.

Elizabeth Tudor, who became Queen Elizabeth I of England, stepped through Traitors' Gate twice and lived to tell the tale. The first time she entered in terror, the prisoner of her sister,

State prisoners entered the Tower of London through Traitors' Gate, on the River Thames.

Queen Mary. The second time she entered in triumph, a queen herself.

What's unusual is that both passages through that famous doorway were described in writing. History generally records what happens on one side or the other of a door, but rarely what happens in the doorway itself.

And that's a pity, because doors have a special magic—the magic of potential. They can open in or out. They can hide or reveal. They can separate places and people or join them together. They can mark a passage from one way of life to another—or from life to death.

When you open the door to your home, you touch the same surface and pass through the same space as family, friends, visitors—and, perhaps, complete strangers who lived in the home before your time.

Think of how many people touch the doors and pass through the doorways of schools, stores, apartment blocks, and office buildings. Who might have stepped through the door of an old house or an ancient temple or a tumbledown barn? What were their lives like? What did they feel when they stood in that doorway?

Feelings are part of the magic of doorways. Think of stepping into a strange classroom on your first day in a new school. Or opening the door to your home after a long time away. Or crawling out through a tent flap into a glorious summer morning by a lake. Excitement, fear, relief, awe—the emotions associated with a place start at the doorway.

A Bedouin policeman lounges in the huge doorway of the Treasury at Petra, in Jordan.

An iron grate blocks a small door in Cape Coast Castle, an old slave fort in Ghana.

In this book, you'll find an assortment of very different doors and doorways, from an oddly shaped opening in an old stone wall to a multistory gateway designed to frighten people. You'll meet some of the people who passed through these doorways or stood and gazed at them in awe, and you'll get a glimpse of their lives, on both sides of the door.

Just open the door and come on in!

DOOR IN THE CLIFF:
Al-Khazneh, Petra

The Bedouin, the desert-dwellers of northern Arabia, tell a story of a great door in the desert. Long ago, they say, a wicked pharaoh, who was also a powerful magician, chased Moses and the Hebrew people out of Egypt and across the Red Sea.

For reasons that make sense only to evil magicians, the pharaoh brought his treasure along on the chase. At the sandstone cliffs of Petra, northeast of the Red Sea, he hid the treasure in a huge stone urn. Then he lifted the urn by magic and set it over a great doorway carved into the cliff itself, far above the reach of non-magical hands.

The urn is still there, and so is the doorway—now called the Pharaoh's Treasury, or al-Khazneh.

ROSE-RED LIGHT AT THE END OF THE TUNNEL

AL-KHAZNEH IS HIDDEN AMONG SANDSTONE CLIFFS that rise out of the stony desert of southern Jordan. You reach it through the Siq, a narrow crack in the cliffs that stretches for

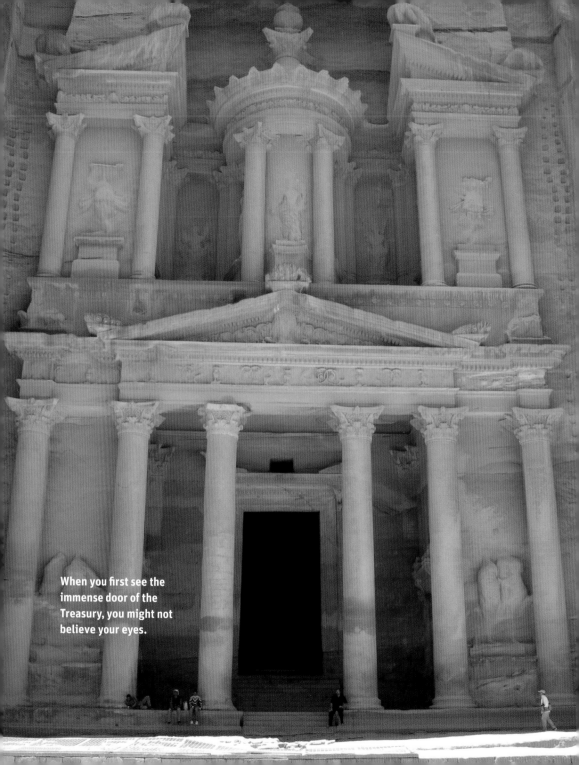

When you first see the immense door of the Treasury, you might not believe your eyes.

1.2 kilometers (three-quarters of a mile).

As you slip into the shade of the Siq, the cooler air is a relief. Touching your hand to the wall, you can feel the smoothness of the sandstone, polished by centuries of winter rains and flash floods. The path ahead curves out of sight, following the twists of the natural split in the rock. Between the towering walls, the golden morning has become a gloomy half-light. As you follow the path, you pass through sections so narrow there is barely enough space for two camels to walk side by side.

It's obvious that this path was traveled by people centuries ago. The walls still contain ancient, carved-out niches, inset with rectangular blocks representing gods. Figures are carved into the walls too, humans and camels, although most of the detail has been erased by time and flood water.

After about 20 long minutes, reflected light breaks through the gloom. You blink at the brightness, then blink again, wondering if your eyes are playing a trick. Directly ahead, framed by the Siq's walls and glowing reddish-peach, is the front of a towering building cut into the side of a cliff.

The first glimpse of the Treasury from within the Siq

Stepping out of the Siq, you stare in amazement across a stretch of sand no wider than a four-lane highway. There stands the Pharaoh's Treasury, as tall as a 12-story building and layered like a wedding cake!

The bottom layer is a giant porch. A few wide steps lead to the sheltered floor of the porch, and a narrower staircase then leads to the great central doorway. Three columns loom on each side of the doorway, hiding small side chambers.

Above the peaked roof of the porch is the second layer: partial roofs on either side and, in the middle, a narrow stone gazebo with the carved figure of a goddess.

The whole construction is decorated with mythical figures, vines, fruit, and stylized rosettes, all carved into the cliff. At the very top is the great stone urn, pockmarked by the bullets of optimistic Bedouin sharpshooters who hoped to crack it open and spill the wicked pharaoh's treasure.

But the urn holds no treasure, and never did.

A DOOR FOR GODS OR GIANTS

THE URN, THE IMMENSE FACADE, and the door itself were all carved into the sandstone cliff by the Nabataeans, wealthy traders in spices and incense

Petra is called the rose-red city because of an 1845 poem, "Petra," by John William Burgon, which ends: "…a rose-red city half as old as time."

Visitors ride through the Siq in a donkey cart. Channels cut by the Nabataeans to carry water can be seen on the walls.

The stone urn on top of the great door is scarred by the bullets of hopeful Bedouins.

who lived a thousand years after Moses. In this hidden valley, they built the city of Petra—and the great Treasury.

The giant doorway is four or five times the height of a man, and wide enough for half a dozen people to enter at once. It looks like a doorway into the mountain itself.

Step through the door—and you enter another world. The room behind the door is far smaller than the facade, although it's still big enough to swallow a medium-sized family house, roof and all. And it's totally bare. The smooth walls are decorated with nothing more than the ribbon pattern of the sandstone. Three small rooms lead off the main room, but nothing remains in any of the rooms to explain how they were used.

Who created al-Khazneh? And when? And why? Until recently, there were no answers to those questions—only guesses. Its construction date was pegged anywhere from 100 BCE to 200 CE. Historians thought it might have been a temple, or a tomb, or even a library.

MODERN SCIENCE MEETS THE TREASURY

IN 2003, JORDANIAN ARCHEOLOGISTS began to excavate in front of the Treasury. Ground-penetrating radar told them something was buried under the debris left by 2000 years of flash floods, but they weren't sure what. When they began digging, they were astonished.

Beneath the Treasury lay an entire lower story of tombs cut into the rock wall. In front of one small tomb, the diggers found a hearth full of ash containing the charred bones of animals

A narrow stairway leads down to one of the tombs below the Treasury.

that had probably been sacrificed. They also found broken bowls, and even—to their great delight—a small stone vessel still holding incense that someone had left as an offering more than 2000 years ago. People had performed ceremonial and religious rites there.

For the archeologists, the most exciting find in what they named the Incense Tomb was the broken pottery. The bowls had been made between 25 BCE and 1 CE. Finally, the first solid clue to the construction date of the Treasury itself!

The evidence of the bowls dates the Incense Tomb to the end of the first century BCE. The larger tombs were built a few years later, and the Treasury came later still. When the Treasury facade was carved, the wide porch and the great doorway cut off parts of the roof decorations of the tombs beneath.

At the ground level of the tombs, the archeologists made a further discovery. The area in front of the tombs had been paved with large, flat stones, forming a plaza that stretched right across the valley to the Siq. In the middle of the plaza, where radar had shown some kind of structure, the archeologists found the base of a massive stone staircase that had once climbed upward to the Treasury door, above the row of tombs.

THE KING WHO LOVED HIS PEOPLE

ARCHEOLOGISTS ARE STILL analyzing the results of the excavations, but already the evidence is painting a new picture of al-Khazneh and its immense doorway.

Early Nabataeans used plain, rectangular blocks to represent their gods. The carved human and animal figures on al-Khazneh show the influence of Egyptian, Greek, and Roman art.

Al-Khazneh was built during the reign of King Aretas IV, who came to the throne in 9 BCE and ruled for 49 years, during the most prosperous period of the Nabataean kingdom. In Nabataean inscriptions, he's called "Aretas, the king, king of the Nabataeans, who loves his people."

The discovery of the tombs proves that the great facade is a mausoleum, an elaborate building constructed to honor the dead. More than a dozen skeletons have been found in the tombs

Archeologists excavate a tomb beneath the Treasury.

beneath al-Khazneh. While we don't know their names, we have clues to who they were.

These people, buried at the height of Petra's prosperity beneath the most spectacular monument in the city, were probably members of the royal family, relatives of King Aretas himself. Among them, perhaps, is the king's first wife, Queen Huldu, who died around the time the later tombs were finished and work began on the great door above them.

The one thing that's certain is the importance of al-Khazneh to the Nabataeans. Everywhere the archeologists dug in the ancient plaza, they found burnt incense, a mark of great honor. They also found an altar, more broken pottery and ceremonial hearths, and burnt animal bones. With all those signs of religious offerings, al-Khazneh was clearly a place of pilgrimage.

AL-KHAZNEH IN ITS GLORY

WHAT MIGHT THE PILGRIMS have experienced 2000 years ago? The first sight of al-Khazneh would have been breathtaking.

The Siq then was just as gloomy as today, but it was paved with smooth stones and lined with carved shrines to Nabataean gods. Dams in the side canyons protected the passage from flash floods and trapped water. Channels and pipes along the sides of the Siq carried water to the city, so the gurgle of running water would have broken the silence of the narrow canyon.

When they emerged from the Siq, weary travelers would have stopped in awe. A paved plaza stretched before them. On its far side, in front of the tombs, people knelt at altars, and the sharp odor of burning incense drifted in the warm air. Above the worshippers

Small oil lamps were found in the tombs beneath the Treasury door.

15

towered the magnificent facade, its carvings sharp-edged in the clear desert light. And in the center, at the top of a huge stone staircase, stood the great doorway itself.

Most pilgrims probably made their offerings in the plaza itself or before the tombs. The wealthy and powerful—perhaps King Aretas himself—might have climbed the great staircase and passed between huge wooden doors into the central chamber to pay their respects to the dead and the gods.

We don't know—yet—exactly what went on in that great chamber beyond the doorway. Perhaps ceremonial feasts were held, like the ones described by the Greek geographer Strabo, who lived about the same time as Aretas IV: "[The Nabataeans] eat their meals in companies consisting of thirteen persons. Each party is attended by two musicians. …No one drinks more than eleven … cupfuls, from separate cups, each of gold."

It's easy to imagine the great empty room behind the door of al-Khazneh, perhaps set with tables and richly colored cushions, echoing to the sounds of harp and flute. The king and his guests—in pleated robes, their hair intricately coiled—feast from delicate, decorated plates in a tribute to the dead. Light flowing in through the huge doorway might glint off a gold cup, raised by a king to honor his lost queen.

AND THEN THERE WERE NONE

IN 106 CE, THE LAST KING of Nabataea died and his kingdom was absorbed peacefully into the Roman Empire. Over the next couple of centuries, Petra changed. Sea routes replaced desert

Door in the Cliff: Al-Khazneh, Petra

In the movie *Indiana Jones and the Last Crusade*, the heroes ride through the Siq to the Treasury, dismount, and run up the steps through the door. With the help of movie magic, however, they end up in the Grail Temple, not the empty stone room of al-Khazneh.

The mysterious room behind the Treasury's door is bare and empty today.

Flash floods washed debris into the valley and buried the Treasury's lower story.

caravans, the incense traders went elsewhere, and the population dwindled.

The beliefs that had inspired pilgrims to burn incense before the Treasury or feast behind its great door gave way to new religions. Three hundred years after the death of Aretas IV, the tomb of another Nabataean king was turned into a Christian church. In the seventh century, the new religion of Islam spread through the old lands of Nabataea. No one came anymore to honor the dead beneath the door of al-Khazneh.

Wars swept through the region, driving more people away. In the 12th century, Christian Crusaders from Europe built a small fort among the ruins of Petra and held it for more than 70 years. If they explored the narrow valley leading to al-Khazneh and entered the door in the cliff, they left no record.

Earthquakes damaged parts of the city, but al-Khazneh, carved into the solid cliff, survived. Looters ventured through the door and hauled away everything of value. Then they too left. Eventually, no one remained in Petra but the occasional Bedouin family, camping in a deserted tomb.

The beautiful facade of al-Khazneh still stood, rarely seen by anyone, protected by its narrow valley from wind and rain.

But nothing could protect it from floods. The Nabataeans' pipes and dams disintegrated, and once again flash floods poured through the Siq and the narrow valley in front of al-Khazneh during the rainy season. Layers of sand and broken rock built up on the valley floor until the tombs beneath the Treasury were buried and forgotten. Only the immense, empty doorway above remained.

The Treasury rediscovered

By 1800, no European had visited Petra in centuries, and even its location had been forgotten. It was called "the lost city of the Nabataeans." Of course, it wasn't really lost. The Bedouin knew exactly where Petra was, but they considered it their private territory, and they didn't welcome strangers.

Then along came Johann Burckhardt, a Swiss scholar and adventurer.

It was 1812, and Arabia was part of the Muslim Ottoman Empire. Christian Europeans weren't encouraged to roam around unsupervised. Burckhardt, 27 years old, had just spent more than two years in Syria, learning Arabic and possibly converting to Islam. Now he was on his way to Cairo, disguised as a Muslim traveler named Sheikh Ibrahim Ibn Abdallah.

Along the way, Burckhardt planned a side trip through the valley called Wadi Mousa, or the Valley of Moses. He had heard rumors of a great ruined city in Wadi Mousa and wanted to see it for himself. To avoid arousing suspicion among the local Bedouin, he told his guide that he had vowed to sacrifice a goat at the tomb of Aaron, the brother of Moses, at the far end of the valley. And so they went, the guide carrying the goat.

Johann Burckhardt dressed as an Arab to travel through Arabia in 1812.

Like travelers of old, Burckhardt approached Petra through the Siq. When he stepped out of the dark passage and saw the Treasury looming above him, he was deeply impressed. This must be the tomb of a prince, he wrote, "and great must have been the opulence of a city, which could dedicate such monuments to the memory of its rulers."

Burckhardt climbed the wide stairs and stepped through the door into the main chamber, as empty then as it is now. He paced out the dimensions of the rooms and studied the decoration on the facade, scribbling down notes later in a journal that he kept well hidden from his suspicious guide. Then they continued down the valley to the main part of the city, the disguised scholar poking into ruined tombs and buildings along the way.

Finally, his exasperated guide accused him of wanting to steal the treasures of the ancients. Burckhardt decided it was time to go. He found a convenient place to sacrifice the goat and then he and his guide camped for the night, dining on part of the sacrifice.

Early the next morning, the two men left Wadi Mousa. Much later, after searching through his reference books, Burckhardt

The United Nations Educational, Scientific and Cultural Organization (UNESCO) keeps a list of places around the world that have been officially designated World Heritage Sites. These are places considered to be of outstanding value to all people.

Some of the sites are natural, such as Australia's Great Barrier Reef or the Grand Canyon National Park in the United States. Others are cultural—things created by humans—such as the Great Wall of China or the Acropolis in Athens.

All eight doorways in this book are part of UNESCO World Heritage Sites.

concluded that the ruined city must be Petra. He never returned to it—but that single day brought the Treasury and the ancient city of Petra back to the knowledge of the outside world.

THE NEW PILGRIMS

TODAY, PETRA AND THE TREASURY are far from lost. Thousands of tourists visit it every year. Hundreds of scholars are trying to unravel its secrets and learn more about the people who carved that great doorway in a cliff.

Al-Khazneh is Petra's best known attraction. People from all parts of the world step through its door to stand in that huge, bare room and listen to the story of the Nabataeans and their rose-red city. Ironically, some of the tour guides telling the story are descended from the Bedouin who guarded the secret of the Pharaoh's Treasury for so many years.

Recent excavations have unearthed an entire layer of tombs beneath the Treasury.

DOOR BETWEEN LIFE AND DEATH:
Castel Sant'Angelo, Rome

The first permanent resident of Castel Sant'Angelo was already dead when he entered its doorway. The mighty Roman emperor Hadrian had been reduced to ashes in an urn. In a solemn funeral procession, his remains were carried across the Tiber River and into Rome's newest, largest, and most spectacular mausoleum, or tomb.

THAT SCENE TOOK PLACE 1900 years ago. Since then, Castel Sant'Angelo has served as tomb and fortress, palace, prison, and museum. Through most of that time, death has lurked near its front door.

BIGGEST AND BEST

IN ROME, FROM 117 TO 138 CE, no one was more important than the emperor, Hadrian. A soldier by training, he ruled for over 20 years. He was famous for traveling throughout his vast empire, often on foot, from Britain in the north to Egypt in the south.

To reach the door of Castel Sant'Angelo, visitors cross this bridge, just as Hadrian planned almost 1900 years ago.

As he grew older, Hadrian began planning a mausoleum worthy of his ashes. It was customary for a Roman emperor to be declared a kind of state god after death, so the mausoleum would be part tomb, part temple. It would also mark the beginning of his own dynasty and serve as a burial place for his heirs.

Hadrian was determined that his would be the biggest, most magnificent mausoleum in Rome. First, he had a new bridge built across the Tiber River from the main part of the city. It swooped over the water on elegant arches, straight to the mausoleum's grand entrance door.

A coin from Hadrian's reign shows us what he looked like.

The mausoleum itself was immense. Its base was a square, each side nearly twice the length of an Olympic swimming pool. On top of the square base was a round building, like a giant drum many stories high. Cypress trees—tall, dark evergreens that symbolize death—were planted in a great mound of earth on its roof.

At the very top stood a statue. An early Roman historian, Dio, described it as a huge bronze likeness of Hadrian driving a chariot pulled by four horses. "It was so large that the bulkiest man could walk through the eye of each

The last Roman emperor whose ashes were carried through the door of Castel Sant'Angelo was Caracalla, who was assassinated in 217 while peeing at the side of a road.

horse," Dio reported, "yet because of the extreme height of the monument persons passing along on the ground below are wont to think that the horses themselves as well as Hadrian are very small."

A GRAND FAREWELL

HADRIAN DIED IN THE SUMMER of 138 CE. Since his mausoleum was unfinished, the emperor had to be buried in a temporary grave. Finally, more than a year later, the imperial funeral could go ahead.

Hadrian's body was removed from its temporary grave and cremated in a public ceremony. Then the ashes were carried in procession to the new mausoleum, along with the ashes of his wife Sabina, who had died shortly before Hadrian, and those of an adopted son who had also died in 138.

Funeral processions for prominent Romans—and no one was more prominent than an emperor—were almost like parades, accompanied by musicians, dancers, mimes, and professional mourning-women. Hadrian's mourners would have included the new emperor and all the important and wealthy people of Rome, as well as officials from other parts of the far-flung empire.

The procession wound through the streets of Rome before

Hadrian's funeral procession would have come through this passage. A statue of the emperor probably stood in the alcove ahead.

crossing the new bridge to the mausoleum's great door, framed by stone blocks and set into marble-clad walls. Torchbearers lit the way as the urns were carried through the door into the dark interior. The long line of mourners walked down a corridor and through a vestibule overseen by a statue of Hadrian himself. Then they climbed up the wide spiral ramp that coils around the cylinder-shaped core of the mausoleum to a room in the very heart of the building. There the urns were left to spend eternity together.

Ironically, Hadrian and Sabina, who shared a room in death, had disliked each other in life and spent as little time together as possible!

TOO GOOD TO WASTE

FOR YEARS, ONLY THE DEAD—Hadrian's successors and their families—and those who came to honor them passed through the mausoleum's door. But Hadrian's mausoleum was too big, too well built, and too conveniently located to be left to the dead alone.

Toward the end of the third century, the peace of the mausoleum was disturbed by the tramp of soldiers marching through the door. The building became part of a defensive wall that encircled the entire city. While Hadrian and his heirs lay in their urns, troops stomped through the halls and up to the roof to keep watch over Rome.

Rome needed watching in those days. Its enemies were closing in. In 537, the Goths, from northeastern Europe, laid

siege to Rome and fought their way right to the mausoleum door. They almost made it past the entrance.

The Goths attacked the mausoleum on the 18th day of the siege. Barricading the heavy door, the outnumbered defenders ran to the roof with their bows and ballistae, powerful weapons shaped like giant crossbows. But the Goths blocked the

Stone cannonballs are still piled behind the outer walls of Castel Sant'Angelo. The rough wall on the right is Hadrian's original mausoleum.

arrows with their long shields and hauled scaling ladders to the base of the walls.

The defenders were in trouble. Their arrows were useless, and the ballistae couldn't be aimed straight down on the Goths climbing their tall ladders. In desperation, the men on the roof knocked down the huge statues of men and horses, smashed them, and dropped heavy, jagged chunks of stone onto the Goths below.

Knocked off their ladders and pummeled by a torrent of rocks, the Goths retreated.

THE ARRIVAL OF THE ANGEL

BY THE LATE SIXTH CENTURY, Rome was a very different place from the city Hadrian had known—and so was his mausoleum. Rome had become a Christian city ruled by the pope, the leader of Catholic Christians. And in 591, the mausoleum earned its current name.

For months, Rome had suffered a terrible plague. As a last resort, Pope Gregory I led a procession through the city, from church to church, asking

On top of the castle, a bronze statue of an angel sheathing his sword commemorates the vision of Pope Gregory in 591.

God to stop the sickness. According to tradition, as he approached the entrance of Hadrian's tomb, he saw a vision: a warrior angel appeared on the roof and, as the pope watched, slid his great sword back into its sheath. The pope took the vision as a sign from God that the plague would soon end—and it did. Since people in the sixth century had no idea what caused or cured infectious diseases, the pope's angel was given credit.

In Roman slang, to tell someone he or she is as beautiful as the Angelo di Castello (the Castel's angel) is the highest form of a compliment.

To show his gratitude, Pope Gregory built a chapel on the spot where he believed he had seen the angel and, beside it, placed a statue of the angel holding the sword. From that time forward, Hadrian's mausoleum was known as Castel Sant'Angelo, the Castle of the Holy Angel.

Hadrian and his dynasty were all but forgotten, and at some point the imperial urns disappeared from the fortress. Now, soldiers paced Castel Sant'Angelo's fortified roof and, in times of danger, soldiers and civilians alike took refuge behind its door—a door to life, not death.

THE POPE'S REFUGE

MOST BUILDINGS CRUMBLE away over time. Castel Sant'Angelo just kept getting bigger and more elaborate—and so did its door.

This 1890s map shows the layers of walls built around Hadrian's mausoleum.

Outer walls were built around the center, and an outer gate guarded the grand door. In the 13th century, the popes chose Castel Sant'Angelo as a safe retreat and added luxurious living quarters. One pope built a backdoor escape route, a fortified passageway called Passetto di Borgo. It was about 800 meters (half a mile) long and led from the pope's headquarters, in the complex of buildings called the Vatican, straight into the Castel.

By then, Castel Sant'Angelo had become an important part of the popes' political and military power. When Pope Sixtus IV died in 1484, his nephew, Girolamo Riario, wanted to make sure that the next pope was chosen from his family. His first step was to seize the Castel.

Or, rather, he sent his young wife to do the job. Caterina Sforza had been married since she was 15 and had already borne several children. She was known and respected in Rome for her beauty, her intelligence, and her ambition.

In 1484, she was 21 years old and pregnant with her fifth child. Nevertheless, she strapped on a sword and led her men through the Castel's door, barricading it shut behind them.

Caterina and her small band occupied Castel Sant'Angelo for weeks while Riario and his family schemed to stay in power. In the end, though, the family's politicking failed. A rival candidate was elected pope, and Caterina had to open the door and give up the Castel to its new master.

THE POPE AND THE GOLDSMITH

LESS THAN 50 YEARS LATER, the Castel's value as a papal refuge was put to its greatest test. In May 1527, in the midst of a complex struggle for power in Europe, Rome was attacked by an army serving Charles V, the Holy Roman Emperor. Pope Clement VII and senior church officials fled from the Vatican down the Passetto di Borgo and through the back door into the safety of Castel Sant'Angelo.

Meanwhile, at the front door, Roman citizens of all ranks struggled to reach safety behind the castle walls. The guards shoved and kicked at the crowd and finally managed to close the iron grate, after about 3000 people had scrambled through. But thousands more were stranded outside.

One of those who got through the door was Benvenuto Cellini. Cellini was a goldsmith, an artist, and a bit of a scoundrel. He and his friends were among the last to make it into the fortress.

The goldsmith joined a crew of bombardiers manning heavy guns on the highest point of the building, the very place where an earlier pope had seen a vision of an angel. This time there was no deliverance from disaster. The invading army terrorized

From the battlements where Benvenuto Cellini watched Rome being attacked, people can now be seen peacefully crossing Hadrian's bridge.

the city. For weeks, soldiers looted Rome, demanded ransom money from wealthy citizens, and tortured and murdered those who couldn't pay.

The pope, Cellini, and the rest of those sheltering in Castel Sant'Angelo watched helplessly as people were slaughtered within sight of the Castel's door—a door that stood, yet again, between life and death.

Eventually, Charles V's commanders regained control of the army and Pope Clement bought peace by paying a huge ransom and giving up some of his territory. Castel Sant'Angelo had kept him safe, as it was supposed to, but that was little comfort to the suffering Romans outside its walls.

In 928, Pope John X was imprisoned in Castel Sant'Angelo by political rivals. The pope died shortly afterward in mysterious circumstances—murdered, according to rumor.

BEHIND LOCKED DOORS

THE LOCKED DOORS of Castel Sant'Angelo did more than keep invaders out. They also kept prisoners in, particularly important people such as cardinals, enemy hostages, and high-ranking prisoners—including Caterina Sforza.

After her husband died, Caterina earned a reputation as a woman who was dangerous to cross. But eventually she ran into someone even more dangerous: Cesare Borgia, an ambitious schemer. Borgia took control of the family lands and locked

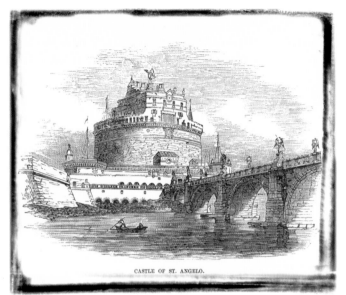

CASTLE OF ST. ANGELO.

Caterina in Castel Sant'Angelo, 15 years after she had held it with a sword and a few men. After a year of misery in the prison's dark, dirty cells, Caterina gave up all claim to rule, and Borgia let her walk out the castle door, a free woman.

Benvenuto Cellini was also escorted through the Castel's door as a prisoner—almost 20 years after he had fled there from the army of Charles V. The goldsmith was charged—falsely, he insisted—with stealing some of the pope's jewels during that long-ago siege.

After months of imprisonment, he attempted a daring escape through the castle's latrines, but only succeeded in breaking his leg. He was recaptured, strapped to a stretcher, and carried back through the door of Castel Sant'Angelo, to a cell "which swam with water, and was full of big spiders and many venomous worms."

Cellini endured several more months as a prisoner before he was released and sent into exile in France. He left the Castel one last time—out the front door, and on his own two legs.

CHANGING TIMES

OVER THE NEXT COUPLE OF CENTURIES, as armies developed bigger guns and more powerful explosives, fortresses were less useful for keeping out enemies. But the door of Castel Sant'Angelo still served to keep people in.

By the 1800s, it was primarily a prison, with hundreds of people crammed into every available space. Many were political prisoners caught up in the long struggle that created the modern nation of Italy from more than a dozen small, squabbling kingdoms and principalities.

In 1870, as part of that struggle, the pope was forced to turn over most of the territory he ruled to the newly formed Italian government. That included Castel Sant'Angelo.

For the next 30 years, soldiers once again marched in and out the door that had once welcomed Hadrian's ashes to their resting place. Finally, in 1901, the ancient, battered fortress was retired from its military role and work began to turn it into a museum.

Since the 1930s, Castel Sant'Angelo has been a museum commemorating 1900 years of Roman history.

BACK THROUGH THE DOOR

TODAY, CASTEL SANT'ANGELO is the second-largest building in Rome—beaten only by another ancient monument, the Colosseum.

You can still follow the path taken by Hadrian's ashes, across the bridge that rests on foundations his engineers built. You

Today, visitors pour through the door where Hadrian's funeral procession once entered.

can enter through the great door where his mourners passed 1900 years ago and see, ahead of you, the spiral ramp to his resting place. You can walk past the vestibule where his statue once stood. But the former emperor would scarcely recognize the place.

Ten great sculpted angels and two saints now guard the length of the bridge. Walls and battlements surround the original mausoleum. The dark cypress trees that once grew on its roof have been replaced by papal apartments and fortifications. On top, in place of a statue of the emperor, is a bronze angel marking the place of Pope Gregory's vision—one of a succession of angel statues that have stood there over the centuries.

Inside the Castel Sant'Angelo, all the ages of the building are on display: Hadrian's spiral ramp, the elegant apartments of the Renaissance popes, the dank cells where thousands of prisoners suffered, and the weapons of the soldiers who defended the Castel Sant'Angelo and Rome itself.

Today, when you step through the door of Castel Sant'Angelo, you step into a long and multilayered past.

DOOR TO THE SKY:
Spruce Tree House, Colorado

Stand in an oddly shaped doorway of Spruce Tree House and look southwestward, out of the great alcove in the cliff, to the wide, windy skies above Mesa Verde. Dark evergreens line the far rim of the canyon above a layered stone cliff. In winter, snow blankets the rock. In summer, heat rises from the canyon walls and wildflowers bloom on the surface of the mesa.

EIGHT CENTURIES AGO, someone applying the last bit of mortar to that doorway might have looked at much the same view.

Spruce Tree House is an ancient cliff dwelling in Mesa Verde National Park, Colorado, in the southwestern United States. It's not so much a house as a small community, built neatly into a massive space below the lip of the canyon. The sandstone of the cliff protects the village on three sides and the slab of overhanging rock—the equivalent of five stories in thickness—shades and shelters it from above.

No one is quite sure why the Ancestral Puebloans built these doorways in a T shape.

Over a hundred small, rectangular rooms fit into the alcove, which is about as deep as the length of a basketball court and a little more than twice as wide. Made of the same pinkish-tan sandstone as the cliff itself, the rooms are layered up to three stories high. Small, round plazas scattered among the houses are actually the roofs of underground chambers, covered with logs and juniper bark and then paved with mud. The chambers, called kivas, were probably used for ceremonial purposes.

One of the minor puzzles of Spruce Tree House is its curious doorways. They are T-shaped, a bit like large, blocky keyholes. Perhaps the shape had religious meaning. Or, as some people suggest, the shape marked a doorway into a public area. Or maybe the builders just thought they would look nice.

To reach their fields, the people of Spruce Tree House had to scramble up a steep path in the cliff to the mesa top above.

PEOPLE OF CLIFFS AND CANYONS

WE CAN'T ASK the builders because they're long gone. But imagine one of them standing in that T-shaped doorway 800 years ago, when 60 to 90 people lived in the alcove's rooms.

modern relatives, Pueblo Native Americans such as the Hopi in north-central Arizona and the Zuni in northwestern New Mexico.

The Ancestral Puebloans lived on Mesa Verde as early as 550 CE. For centuries they built their houses on the mesa itself, the relatively flat plateau above the canyon. They grew corn, beans, and squash, hunted deer and smaller animals, gathered wild fruits and plants, and raised turkeys in pens. They made elegantly decorated pots, yucca-fiber sandals, and warm robes of woven turkey feathers.

Eight centuries ago, dishes of corn like these sat next to the cooking fires of Spruce Tree House.

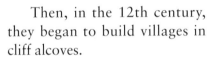

Then, in the 12th century, they began to build villages in cliff alcoves.

By studying tree rings in wooden beams used in the cliff houses, scientists have determined when many of the dwellings were built. Spruce Tree House, like most of them, was built in several stages, from the late 1100s to about 1280.

And then, within a few years, the people left. By 1300, the cliff houses of Mesa Verde were all but empty.

THE COWBOY IN THE SNOW

FOR ALMOST 600 YEARS, as far as we know, no one walked through the T-shaped doorway into one of the crumbling rooms. Spruce Tree House stood vacant.

The descendants of the Ancestral Puebloans had moved to new homes south of Mesa Verde. Navajo and Ute people had come into the area, but they avoided the old buildings. They called them the houses of the dead.

Eventually, Europeans arrived, but they were more interested in valuable minerals and rich farmland than in the deep canyons and dry mesa tops. Although a few travelers had reported seeing ancient buildings in the Mesa Verde area, their reports attracted little attention.

Then, near the end of the 19th century, the Wetherill family brought the cliff dwellings to the attention of the world.

The family was made up of B. K. Wetherill, his wife Marion, five sons and a daughter, and son-in-law Charlie Mason. They lived on a ranch in the Mancos Valley and sometimes grazed their cattle on Mesa Verde.

On a cold December day in 1888, Richard Wetherill, the oldest son, was riding on the mesa top with Charlie Mason and

Richard Wetherill, a Colorado rancher, rediscovered and named Spruce Tree House in 1888.

Richard Wetherill, the man who rediscovered Spruce Tree House, died June 22, 1910. He was shot to death, apparently by a Navajo man in a dispute over a horse.

a Ute friend, looking for stray cattle. They picked their way through the juniper and piñon forest of the mesa top until they broke into the open at the edge of a side canyon. The men stopped, transfixed. Across the canyon, tucked into the cliff face, stood an ancient city.

Richard and Charlie forgot about stray cattle. Leaving their horses with their friend, they scrambled down into the canyon and climbed up the far side. The broad ledge contained at least 150 rooms, their floors still littered with abandoned tools and unbroken pots. It almost felt as if the cliff-dwellers had left only a short while ago. On the spot, they named it Cliff Palace.

Wild with excitement, the men split up to search for more. Richard crossed the mesa top and found another canyon nearby. Under the lip of the cliff was a second dwelling-place almost as big as the first. Because a tree grew up from the canyon floor next to the cliff, providing a natural ladder, Richard named his new discovery Spruce Tree House. The tree, later cut down, was actually a Douglas fir.

Richard Wetherill may have been the first person to walk through that T-shaped door in Spruce Tree House in almost six centuries. But he certainly wasn't the last.

LIFE RETURNS TO SPRUCE TREE HOUSE

THE WETHERILL BROTHERS, along with a succession of partners, explored dozens of cliff houses over the next decades. They also collected artifacts, which they sold to private enthusiasts and museums. And they set up tours.

For 20 dollars a person—a hefty sum in the 1890s—the brothers brought tourists to Spruce Tree House and other sites. Passing through the ancient doorways, excited visitors wandered through the abandoned rooms.

One of their paying guests was Baron Gustaf Nordenskiöld, a young Swede trained in geology. In 1891, he came to the Wetherill ranch to see the cliff dwellings and was entranced. He hired Richard to help him excavate several sites, including Spruce Tree House.

When he returned to Europe, Nordenskiöld published a book about the cliff-dwellers of Mesa Verde, which introduced the spectacular buildings to an international audience. He also took a large collection of artifacts back to Europe with him, most of which ended up in a museum in Finland.

Gustaf Nordenskiöld was only 22 when he came to visit the Mesa Verde sites and stayed to excavate many of them.

One of Nordenskiöld's photographs from 1891 shows Richard's younger brothers, John and Al, sitting in a room in Spruce Tree

Wetherill brothers John and Al prepare lunch in one of the rooms at Spruce Tree House in 1891. A T-shaped door is visible in the back wall.

House. The photo shows a distinctive T-shaped door in the wall behind the brothers. A shovel leans against the outer wall, and jackets and other gear are strewn on ledges. A haunch of meat hangs from a protruding post behind the brothers, who appear to be preparing a meal in the ancient house.

POT-HUNTERS AND SCIENTISTS

THE WETHERILLS UNDERSTOOD the importance and fragility of the cliff houses. If they didn't treat them as carefully as modern archeologists would, that's because archeology was still a young science. Most professional archeologists of the time were no more careful.

And they did try to protect the sites. As early as 1890, B.K. Wetherill wrote to the Smithsonian Institution, an agency charged with protecting the American cultural heritage: "We are particular to preserve the buildings, but fear, unless the Govt. sees proper to make a national park of the canons, including Mesa Verde, that the tourists will destroy them."

Ten years later, government officials and local residents had become concerned about Spruce Tree House and other buildings in the area. Tourists swarmed through the ancient doorways and stamped carelessly through the houses.

The end of a ladder sticks up from a kiva entrance. The uneven walls at the back fit the roof of the alcove.

The alcove near the top of the cliff looks small from a distance, but it's big enough to hold a whole community.

Pot-hunters—people who raid archeological sites for valuable artifacts—were making off with pots, tools, jewelry, and even human bones to sell.

By then, a local guide had built a cabin near Spruce Tree House for the comfort of his guests, who happily clambered about dislodging rocks from the stone walls and poking through the rubble on the floor in search of interesting relics. Some even left garbage behind or scribbled on the walls.

Finally, in 1906, the U.S. government created Mesa Verde National Park. Gradually, scientists began to take over from pot-hunters.

Jesse Fewkes stands outside Mesa Verde's first museum—a cabin near Spruce Tree House.

DR. FEWKES BUILDS A HOUSE

SOON AFTER THE PARK was created, Dr. Jesse Walter Fewkes was sent to examine the sites. The government wanted to learn what, exactly, it had undertaken to protect. When Fewkes stepped through the doorway of Spruce Tree House, he rolled up his sleeves and set to work.

In May and June 1908, Fewkes and his team cleared out years of rubbish. They repaired walls that were near collapse and built channels to direct water away from the buildings. They also built trails, labeled interesting features, and constructed a new and easier approach to the alcove. Although the site had been excavated by the Wetherills and picked over by almost two decades of pot-hunters and tourists, Fewkes and his crew found several hundred bits of pottery, tools, and other specimens in the rubble.

By the end of June, Fewkes reported that he had turned Spruce Tree House into a site that would provide a fine educational experience. Even before the work was complete, he began to tell visitors about Spruce Tree House and the people who had lived there.

The Ancestral Puebloans used fibers from the leaves of yucca plants for everything from sandal straps to rope ladders. Yucca is still used, in products such as shampoo and root beer. The fibers even make a handy, natural dental floss.

QUESTIONS AND ANSWERS

A CENTURY HAS PASSED since Jesse Fewkes rebuilt Spruce Tree House. Millions of visitors have stood in the alcove, puzzled over the T-shaped doorway where the door's builder once stood and looked out to the sky above Mesa Verde. And still questions remain.

Why did the Ancestral Puebloans build Spruce Tree House? Why did they move away from villages on the mesa top and build new homes in the side of a cliff? And why did they leave those beautiful stone buildings forever, after only a few generations?

By analyzing the tree rings in beams like the ones supporting this opening into Spruce Tree House, scientists determined the age of the cliff dwelling.

Did some kind of natural disaster drive them away? Were they attacked by outsiders? Or did something else happen?

Science is beginning to suggest some answers—and raise new questions.

We now know that the Mesa Verde area suffered a terrible drought in the last years of the 13th century, when people left Spruce Tree House. The T-shaped doorway might have looked over dry brown grass and dying trees in those years, or over the blackened remains of wildfires that burned both crops and forest.

Scientists have learned about the Ancestral Puebloans' diet by studying bits of food left in ancient cooking pots and animal bones discarded in garbage piles. They've even analyzed the contents of coprolites—ancient human poop. There is some evidence that people weren't eating well in those years—less corn and more wild plants in their diet, and fewer bones from big, meaty animals like deer. In one location, the people even appear to have eaten corncobs, which they would normally have kept for fuel. Perhaps the drought was making the fields less productive or the land was growing less fertile.

Science may provide more answers. Or perhaps the answers lie elsewhere, outside science and written history.

TALES TOLD BY THE FIRE

ANOTHER KIND OF HISTORY is oral tradition—tales passed from generation to generation to keep the story of a people alive without writing it down. The modern Puebloans' stories link them with the ancient cliff-dwellers. Many of the stories are sacred and are not shared with outsiders, but a few have been recorded. These traditional tales offer clues to the past.

In 1883, an old Hopi man told the story of his clan's long-ago wanderings, when they packed all their belongings and went in search of a new place to plant their crops. In a deep canyon, they came across strange marks—odd footprints, and hand- and toe-holds that led to a cavern near the top of a steep cliff.

At first they planned to use the cavern to store crops, but it was so big and so well sheltered that they decided to build a great house—a many-roomed dwelling much like Spruce Tree House. They lived in the cavern contentedly for many years.

Then relatives from the lands they had left long ago found them. The cliff-dwellers grew lonely for their relations and eventually decided to rejoin the rest of the clan. They packed up

Today tourists explore the courtyards and rooms where, long ago, children played and families ate and slept.

their belongings and left the great house in the cavern behind.

Perhaps the last lived-in days of Spruce Tree House looked like that story. Perhaps the last person to stand in the T-shaped doorway and look out over the mesa was looking toward a new home, and family—in happy anticipation, not in hunger or desperation.

DOOR TO WISDOM:
Sankoré Mosque, Timbuktu

Sand laps at the door of Sankoré Mosque, in the northeastern quarter of Timbuktu. It's the warm golden sand of a fine beach, but there is no ocean here—just the great ocean of sand that is the Sahara Desert.

TIMBUKTU SITS ON THE SOUTHERN SHORE of that desert, a port for the camel caravans that have carried goods and people back and forth across the Sahara for centuries. The city was founded about a thousand years ago. According to one legend, a woman named Buktu discovered a well where Timbuktu now stands and used its water to grow crops such as watermelon.

Then the Tuareg, who were and are the herdsmen and traders of the Sahara, built homes around the well and used the new settlement as a place to store and trade goods, rest their camels, and assemble their caravans. Soon Timbuktu was an important link in the trade routes between central Africa and the Mediterranean.

Sankoré, Timbuktu's oldest mosque, was built in the late

People have been stepping through the door of Sankoré Mosque for more than eight centuries.

1100s, in the neighborhood where Timbuktu's wealthy Muslim traders lived. For more than 800 years, Muslim people, who follow the religion of Islam, have entered through its heavy wooden door—to pray, to learn, to teach, to discuss ideas, and to help each other.

WALLS THAT MELT LIKE SUGAR

SANKORÉ MOSQUE'S DOOR is set in an elegant wall of mud. The rounded walls, towers, and swooping staircases are made of banco, a kind of clay brick strengthened by adding fiber such as rice straw. It's a traditional building material near the wide floodplain of the Niger River, where there's little stone but plenty of mud and clay.

The disadvantage of banco is that it melts in the rain—fortunately, a rare occurrence in Timbuktu. Even without rain, however, banco crumbles slowly from wind erosion and traffic vibration, so the walls need frequent repair. The mosque's imam (religious leader) keeps an eye on the building's condition. When repairs are needed, he appeals to worshippers for contributions of money or materials.

The elegant walls of the mosque are made of mud.

A close-up of a door into Sankoré Mosque shows its decorative metal plates and the mud bricks of the wall.

Once everything is ready, the whole community turns out for a day to help with the repair job.

Tall buildings need special measures. Like quills on a porcupine, boards stick out of Sankoré's minaret—a tower where an official calls people to pray. The boards provide a handy place for masons to stand while they work on the 15-meter (45-foot) walls.

The mosque's wooden doors are reinforced and decorated with elaborate metal plates. Behind the doors are plain walls and heavy columns holding up the roof, with mats on the floor for winter prayers. In summer, the faithful gather in the square courtyard, open to the sky, at the heart of Sankoré Mosque.

JUDGES AND WISE MEN

SANKORÉ, LIKE MOST MOSQUES, was always a place of learning as well as a place to pray. Children whose parents could spare them from work were sent to the mosque to memorize the verses of the Koran, the holy book of Islam, and to learn Arabic, the language in which it was written. As Timbuktu became prosperous, more and more children trooped through the door of Sankoré each day to sit at the feet of the imam and recite their lessons.

And Timbuktu became very prosperous. By the 13th century, great caravans—with up to 40,000 camels in one group—carried salt from mines in the desert south to markets in Timbuktu. There it was sold to merchants who carried it farther south, to the salt-poor interior of Africa.

The sand that blows in from the Sahara and drifts up against the walls and doors of Sankoré Mosque is raising the ground around it. Doorways that were once well above the ground are now level with it and may soon be below it.

Goods moved in the other direction too. Gold from the river valleys south of the desert was traded, often for salt, and loaded on camels for transport to northern Africa and all the countries clustered around the Mediterranean. Northbound caravans also carried food and other supplies to the miners, and slaves for sale in the Sahara itself, Egypt, northern Africa, and even Europe. Everything was packed and unpacked, bought and sold in the markets of Timbuktu, and every exchange brought profit to the city's merchants.

As the traffic across the desert grew, so did the traffic through the door of Sankoré Mosque. Students came from outside Timbuktu to study there. In turn, more teachers flocked to the mosque in search of students as well as the chance to learn from each other.

Sankoré district also became the home of a flourishing book industry. In the Middle Ages, before the days of printing presses, many thousands of books were copied by hand and beautifully decorated with abstract patterns or hand-drawn maps and pictures. Many of the books found their way through the door of Sankoré into the mosque's growing library.

THE UNIVERSITY OF SANKORÉ

SOME OF THE BOOKS copied in Sankoré studios were imported to Timbuktu from other centers of Islamic learning, but many were the original work of local scholars. By the 15th century, Sankoré Mosque had become the hub of a full-fledged university.

Every day, students passed through the doorway of Sankoré Mosque to sit around their teacher in a corner of the courtyard or among the columns of the mosque's quiet interior.

Universities in the medieval Islamic world were very different from modern Western universities. There were no great buildings, no central administration, and no fee schedules. Students came to study with individual scholars and paid them with gifts. In the great days of Sankoré university, a student might also work for his teacher. When he finished studying with that teacher, he paid a fee—a set amount of grain or other food, and often a slave.

The most advanced level of education at Sankoré, the equivalent of a doctorate degree today, would take a student 10 years of study.

All students at Sankoré university studied the Koran and learned Arabic. In addition, they might study literature, logic, mathematics, natural science, astronomy, or history.

At its peak, in the 15th and 16th centuries, as many as 25,000 students and teachers assembled in Timbuktu around Sankoré Mosque. They came from all around the Muslim world, including many of the famous places of Islamic scholarship, as far away as Fez in Morocco or Cairo in Egypt.

Children still come to Sankoré Mosque to learn the Koran, using wooden slates like these instead of notebooks.

THE QADI AND HIS STRING

IN THE LATE 16TH CENTURY, one of the most famous scholars of Sankoré strode through the door of the mosque with a bit of string and gave the place a makeover.

Aqib ben Umar, who lived from 1505 to 1583, served as qadi, or judge, for the whole city of Timbuktu. He was also imam of Sankoré Mosque and rector of Sankoré university—a very powerful person.

Late in life, the qadi made a pilgrimage to Mecca, the birthplace of the Prophet Muhammed, the founder of Islam. While there, he obtained permission to measure the Kaaba, the most holy shrine of Islam. Using a long cord, he measured the exact width and length of the Kaaba, marking them on his cord. Then he carried the cord back home to Timbuktu.

Aqib ben Umar took his marked cord into Sankoré Mosque, staked out the dimensions of the Kaaba, and had the interior of the mosque, behind the door and the outside walls, rebuilt so that it was the same width and length as the Kaaba. Despite more than 400 years of repairing and rebuilding Sankoré's mud-brick walls, its sanctuary still matches the holy shape the qadi marked out with his piece of string.

THE EXILE OF THE SCHOLARS

THE GREAT DAYS OF SANKORÉ UNIVERSITY came to an end soon after the death of Aqib ben Umar.

For two centuries, Timbuktu had belonged to the Songhai empire, based along the Niger River, but in 1590 an army

Sankoré Mosque's famed qadi, Aqib ben Umar, modeled its interior space on the Kaaba of Mecca, seen here surrounded by modern pilgrims.

People continue to pray and study in Sankoré Mosque, as Muslims have done for many generations.

from Morocco in northern Africa defeated the Songhai and occupied Timbuktu. After three years of struggling to control the city, the Moroccan pasha, or governor, decided he'd had enough. The problem, as he saw it, was the intellectuals associated with Sankoré Mosque, who led a quiet resistance to the pasha's rule.

In the fall of 1593, he rounded up the teachers, scholars, and imams of the Sankoré district and threw them into jail. In 1594, after five months in prison, the prisoners were exiled to Morocco, forced under guard and in chains to cross a vast desert. Few returned.

The sunny courtyards and cool, dark halls of Sankoré Mosque were empty of students and the air was no longer filled with voices tossing ideas back and forth. People entered the door of the mosque weighed down with fear and grief, not eager for learning. Life in Timbuktu ground to a halt—markets were empty, workshops abandoned.

Eventually, life returned to Timbuktu. Merchants opened their shops and artisans returned to their workbenches. After several years, some of the scholars made their way back to Sankoré Mosque and students again came to the door in search of teachers. But not as many as before. The university of Sankoré never entirely recovered from the exile of the intellectuals.

MIRAGE IN THE DESERT

THE GLORY DAYS OF TIMBUKTU were over by the 17th century. New and easier sea routes stole much of its trade. The great

Sand drifting against the mosque's walls is a serious threat to the ancient building.

Poles sticking out of
Sankoré's minaret give
masons repairing the
walls a place to stand.

empires of central Africa dwindled and disappeared. And the Sahara expanded relentlessly into the forests and fields that once surrounded Timbuktu and piled in drifts against the door of its oldest mosque.

The city slowly settled into a new life as a town on the edge of an ocean of sand. In Europe, however, the legend of Timbuktu lived on. Since the Middle Ages, rumor had painted it as a city of gold, unimaginable wealth, and brilliant scholars.

In the 19th century, several Europeans risked their lives, and some died, trying to reach Timbuktu. The fact that non-Muslims were not welcome in Timbuktu or any of the lands around it only added to its allure.

Repair days at Sankoré and the other Timbuktu mosques are festive occasions. The workers are entertained with tom-tom drums and flute music by griots, traditional traveling poet-musicians.

When a few Europeans finally reached Timbuktu in the late 1820s and early 1830s, they were deeply disappointed. The glittering city of legend was a dusty desert town, and the gold had moved elsewhere. A couple of the European visitors found their way through the door of Sankoré Mosque to discover the remains of its ancient library, but to most of them Sankoré was just another crumbling building among many.

A NEW KIND OF TREASURE

THE DISAPPOINTED 19TH-CENTURY VISITORS didn't know what they were looking at. Sankoré Mosque was still the heart and soul of its community. The doorway of Sankoré Mosque saw a constant stream of people, coming to pray, to listen to the imam's words of wisdom, to gather with friends and relatives, or to seek refuge in times of trouble.

Today, it remains a busy spot. Although few non-Muslims are allowed through the doorway, people from around the world come to admire the exterior of the ancient building, with its swooping staircase, sloped minaret, and brass-bound door.

In 1755, the minaret of Sankoré Mosque was knocked down in an earthquake. The repairs are still visible if you know where to look. In Lisbon, Portugal, the same massive earthquake destroyed 85 percent of the buildings and killed up to 90,000 people.

Muslim visitors and locals step through the door to worship among the columns in a space exactly the same size as the holy Kaaba of Mecca. And a few children still come to the mosque each day to recite verses of the Koran and write with charcoal on wooden slates, just as children did centuries ago.

The university of Sankoré lives on too, in a way. Much of the mosque's library was destroyed more than 400 years ago when the intellectuals were expelled, but the citizens of Timbuktu have honored the city's tradition of learning. Many families have kept private libraries safe for all those centuries. Now their books—perhaps 300,000 of them—are gradually being collected, restored, and preserved.

The shoes of those who have come to pray wait outside the mosque doors.

The institution that is caring for the books of Timbuktu, the Ahmed Baba Center, is named for a man who knew the door

of Sankoré Mosque better than most. Ahmed Baba taught at Sankoré university during its peak, a revered teacher who wrote dozens of books. He was among the scholars driven away by the pasha in 1594. After 14 years in exile, Ahmed Baba stepped back through the door of Sankoré Mosque and resumed teaching. Like Timbuktu itself, and its treasured mosque, he was a survivor.

DOOR TO DISHONOR:
Traitors' Gate, London

Anne Boleyn, the second wife of Henry VIII of England, passed through the riverside archway called Traitors' Gate twice. The first time, Anne arrived in a royal barge with all her attendants to live in luxury in the Tower of London while she prepared for her wedding to the king. Three years later, she was escorted through Traitors' Gate by guards. Anne had been arrested for treason. Seventeen days after that, she was executed.

TRAITORS' GATE IS THE MOST FAMOUS doorway into the Tower of London—and the last glimpse of freedom for many prisoners. But it didn't acquire its fearsome reputation or its current name until almost two centuries after it was built. Originally, it was known as the Water Gate.

The Tower of London has been a royal residence, a fortress, an armory, and a prison in its thousand-year history. Today the huge collection of buildings, still surrounded by massive walls,

Traitors' Gate, once called the Water Gate, is still under water when the tide is high.

is no longer a feared symbol of royal power. Now the Tower is one of the major tourist destinations in Britain. And everyone who visits wants to see Traitors' Gate.

SAILING THROUGH THE WALLS

CONSTRUCTION ON THE TOWER OF LONDON began shortly after the Norman conquest of England in 1066. William the Conqueror, the new king of England, needed to control the capital city of London, so he built a tall fortified tower to intimidate its citizens. Later kings added walls, more buildings and fortifications, and living quarters for the royal family, servants, and all the people who ran the kingdom.

In 1275, King Edward I began turning the Tower of London into a strong fortress, surrounded by a double set of walls with a moat between. A fortified entrance to the Tower was added on the side where it bordered the River Thames.

Named St. Thomas's Tower, the new entrance was a large gatehouse with towers at both ends and a giant archway between them at river level. A second story above the arch held the king's sleeping quarters. A huge grate called a portcullis could be lowered to block the entrance. When it was raised, boats and barges could sail through the gate to a quay (pronounced "key"), a riverside wharf.

A large, well-guarded water gate was a useful thing in those days. River transport was simpler and cheaper than hauling goods by horse and cart through the narrow, twisting streets of the city. Passengers also traveled by boat if they could afford to, avoiding the foul-smelling streets. The royal family often boated between their residences along the river, as well as to the Palace of Westminster, where government business took place.

Edward I was nicknamed Edward Longshanks, meaning long legs. He was tall for his time, about 188 centimeters (6 feet, 2 inches)— perhaps 23 centimeters (9 inches) taller than the average man of the day.

The modern entry to Traitors' Gate, seen at low tide: St. Thomas's Tower, with Traitors' Gate beneath, is the low building behind the walkway.

ENTRY TO THE TRAITORS GATE

From the turrets of St. Thomas's Tower, guards could see and, if necessary, shoot anyone entering or leaving Traitors' Gate without permission.

Cash on the barrel

SOME OF THE GOODS that arrived at the Water Gate were extremely valuable. Records show that in 1322 King Edward II had money moved from Westminster into the Tower—by the barrelful!

In those days, there were no credit cards or bank accounts to make transferring money easy. You had to carry cash from one place to another, usually in the form of coins.

Edward hired 24 porters to carry 52 barrels of money from the treasury to the quay at Westminster. Two barges and four boats transported the barrels to the Water Gate. Then the porters unloaded them onto the quay and hauled them up to a chapel in a high tower. The old documents tell how the transfer happened and what it cost, but they don't explain why the king went to all that trouble. However, we can guess. Early in 1322, King Edward marched his army north to put down a serious rebellion. It's likely that he locked his money in the Tower, the most secure place in London, to keep it safe from the rebels' allies while he was out of town.

Money wasn't the only thing Edward II kept locked up in the Tower of London. Like most castles, the Tower was also used as a prison, particularly for high-ranking prisoners. State prisoners were often delivered to the Tower by river, through the Water Gate. Transporting political prisoners through the streets of London was risky because supporters might organize a riot or an escape.

After Edward II squashed the rebellion, he threw one of its leaders, Roger Mortimer, the Earl of March, into the Tower.

Less than two years later Mortimer escaped—not through the Water Gate, but over it! He climbed across an arch connected to St. Thomas's Tower and then lowered himself on a smuggled length of rope to a boat waiting in the river.

A RIGHT ROYAL CUSTOM

THE TOWER OF LONDON and the Water Gate were an important part of a happier royal practice. For 300 years, from the time of Edward I, it was traditional for kings and queens to spend some time in the Tower of London before major ceremonies such as coronations or royal weddings.

Most arrived by boat, and the passage through the Water Gate marked the beginning of a new life as king or queen of England. On the big day, they emerged on the landward side, then rode through the city streets to Westminster.

The custom had advantages. First, the new monarch could prepare in privacy and then make a grand entrance on the day of

Traitors' Gate from inside the Tower: Edward I once had a bedroom in the living quarters above the gate.

the ceremony. And second, the Tower, designed as a fortress more than a palace, was the safest of the royal residences. The days before a coronation—the religious ceremony where the monarch formally received the crown—could be very dangerous indeed.

Richard III knew exactly how dangerous. He became king by deposing his own nephew, Edward V, before the boy could be crowned. When Richard arrived at the Water Gate in the royal barge on July 4, 1483, to prepare for his own coronation, Edward and his younger brother were either locked up in the Tower or had already been murdered.

THE BOYS IN THE TOWER

THE STORY OF EDWARD and his brother Richard, Duke of York, is one of the saddest and most mysterious of the many stories associated with the Water Gate and the Tower of London.

The boys were the sons of King Edward IV. Young Edward was 12 when his father died in April 1483, and Richard was just 9.

Because Edward was too young to govern on his own, his uncle Richard, Duke of Gloucester, was his guardian and Lord Protector—the title given to someone who rules on behalf of a child monarch. Richard of Gloucester and the queen's family argued over who would control the throne. In May, the Lord Protector took Edward to the Tower, explaining

The archway of Traitors' Gate is big enough for two double-decker London buses to park under it.

81

St. Thomas's Tower, which surrounds Traitors' Gate, was named for St. Thomas à Becket, an archbishop who was once in charge of the Tower of London. Becket was murdered in 1170 after a dispute with King Henry II, by knights who were loyal to the king.

that he wanted to keep the boy safe while awaiting his coronation, set for June 22.

The queen fled into sanctuary at Westminster Abbey with her other children. Around the middle of June, Richard persuaded her to let the young Duke of York move to the Tower to keep his brother Edward company. The boy was brought by boat, entering through the Water Gate beneath St. Thomas's Tower.

Young Richard of York may have been excited when he docked at the quay. The Tower's royal apartments had been a home to him when his father was alive, and he was going to join his brother and playmate. He was too young to understand the struggle for power. Edward, though, was sad and worried.

He was right to worry. Already, enemies of the boys were spreading rumors that their parents had not been properly married. A few days after Richard of York joined his brother in the Tower, the two boys were declared illegitimate. That meant that young Edward could not be king, and his uncle Richard, the Lord Protector, became heir to the throne.

On July 6, Richard of Gloucester rode through the streets of London, on his way to be crowned Richard III, king of England.

And what happened to the boys? No one knows for sure. A few people reported seeing two children in the Tower garden or behind barred windows in the days after the Duke of York joined his brother. And then there were no further sightings.

People at the time, and most historians today, assume they were killed sometime that summer or autumn, perhaps even before Richard's coronation. However, no bodies were found at the time and no announcement of their deaths was issued. They simply disappeared.

Two centuries later, workmen found the skeletons of two young boys buried in a chest beneath a staircase in the Tower. The bones, assumed to be the remains of the princes, were reburied in Westminster Abbey.

King Henry VIII sent many people through Traitors' Gate to their deaths, including his wife Anne Boleyn, mother of Queen Elizabeth I.

TRAITORS' GATE GETS ITS NAME

RICHARD III HELD THE THRONE for barely two years before his distant cousin, Henry Tudor, defeated Richard's army in 1485 and took the throne as Henry VII. Richard was killed in the final battle.

It was under the Tudors, the royal dynasty founded by Henry VII, that the Water Gate came to be known as Traitors' Gate. The Tudors made plenty of enemies, and quite a few of them were shipped down the river and through the gate to be locked in the Tower. Some were executed there.

Henry VIII, famous for marrying six times, disposed of two of his wives through Traitors' Gate.

One of the wives who suffered that fate was Henry's second wife, Anne Boleyn. Her first visit to the Tower had been a happy occasion. Early in Henry VIII's reign, the Tower of London was still used mainly as a royal residence and the place where kings and queens stayed before important ceremonies. When Anne Boleyn arrived at the Water Gate in the spring of 1533, it was to prepare for her wedding.

This plaque is a modern addition. The gate needed no sign for those taken through as prisoners.

But on May 2, 1536, when she was transported back through the same gate, she was accused of having had an affair with another man. When you're married to a monarch, adultery—having an affair—is high treason. The charges were probably false, but Anne was nevertheless convicted of treason. Henry was already courting his next wife, Jane Seymour, by the time Anne's head was cut off 17 days later.

Jane Seymour died, shortly after giving birth to Henry's son, and the king divorced his fourth wife, Anne of Cleves. His fifth wife was Catherine Howard, who was only about 19 years old when she was put on a barge for her final journey. Like Anne Boleyn, she was accused of adultery and condemned to death for treason. As the barge passed beneath London Bridge on its way to Traitors' Gate, the terrified young queen would have seen the head of the man accused of being her lover stuck on a spike over the bridge gate.

A PRINCESS BEATS THE ODDS

NOT EVERYONE WHO PASSED through Traitors' Gate died in the Tower. Elizabeth, the daughter of Henry and Anne Boleyn, went through that doorway twice—once as a prisoner and once as queen.

The first time was in 1554, when her half-sister Mary was queen. Mary had just put down a rebellion and suspected that Elizabeth had been part of the conspiracy. The 20-year-old princess arrived through Traitors' Gate—probably certain that she would be executed in the Tower as her mother had been.

Queen Elizabeth I, years after being forced through Traitors' Gate as a prisoner.

85

Inside Traitors' Gate, stairs allow boat passengers to climb onto the quay, even at low tide.

Stepping onto the quay, Elizabeth declared, "Here landeth as true a subject, being a prisoner, as ever landed at these steps...." She then sat down on the steps of the quay in the pouring rain and refused to move until the lieutenant of the Tower—and the rain—persuaded her inside.

Elizabeth spent two months in the Tower before her supporters convinced the queen that there was no evidence against her. However, just to be safe, Mary sent her sister to live outside London, well away from court and potential conspirators.

The next time she came to the Tower, Mary had died and Elizabeth was about to be crowned queen herself. In January 1559, Elizabeth spent the week before her coronation in the Tower, preparing for the event. This time, she chose to enter through Traitors' Gate. If the gate was good enough for an innocent princess, she famously said, it was good enough for a queen.

CHANGING TIMES AND CHANGING USES

ELIZABETH I NEVER USED THE TOWER as a residence again—no doubt it had too many painful memories for her—but, like her father and half-sister, she sent plenty of prisoners there. So did her successors, James I and Charles I. But fewer and fewer

Today, modern buildings dwarf both Traitors' Gate and the Tower of London.

Some prisoners lived in relative comfort. This is one of the rooms assigned Sir Walter Raleigh, who wrote a history of the world while locked in the Tower.

entered through Traitors' Gate.

At some point, the old gate fell into disuse and was closed. In 1663, when a new armory and warehouse were being built within the Tower of London, Traitors' Gate was reopened so that building materials could be delivered by river.

That may have been the last time the gate was used as an entrance to the Tower. For most of the 18th century, the archway housed a huge waterwheel. Machinery to manufacture guns had been installed in St. Thomas's Tower. The waterwheel powered it, and also pumped water for the Tower's firefighting system. In 1806, the waterwheel was replaced by a steam engine.

Today, Traitors' Gate is a relic of the past. Boats and barges no longer glide through it to unload royal passengers, barrels of money, or frightened prisoners. In fact, the archway is now blocked off from the river by a raised walk, although water still flows beneath the walk and through the gate.

On busy days, visitors crowd along the walkway, staring down at the arch through which so much regal and tragic history has passed.

6 DOOR TO POWER:
Holy Antechamber, Moscow

Six doors open into the Kremlin's Holy Antechamber. Three are decorative fakes, leading nowhere. The others lead to three vital places in Russia's past and present: the Grand Kremlin Palace, the Faceted Hall, and the Red Porch, a ceremonial staircase down to the square at the heart of the Kremlin.

IN FACT, THE HOLY ANTECHAMBER is itself a doorway—and what a doorway!

It's a rectangular room with a swooping, white vaulted ceiling, the edges trimmed in gold. The doors are framed by pillars and porticos of white stone, decorated with intricate gold designs. Gilt chandeliers hang from the ceiling and matching gilt lamps dot the ornate walls. The bits of wall not filled with grand doorways are covered with murals showing biblical scenes or moments from Russian history.

The Kremlin itself is a central part of Russian history. The walls of this great fortress at the core of Moscow enclose cathedrals, palaces, towers, armories, and other buildings. The

The coronation processions of Russian tsars passed from the Holy Antechamber and the Palace of Facets, extreme left, to the Cathedral of the Assumption, center.

Kremlin has been the seat of government for tsars, dictators, and elected presidents. Today it serves as the official residence and public offices of the president of Russia, and houses museums as well.

Over the centuries, the Kremlin has taken a beating. Its buildings have been bombed, burned, pillaged, torn down, and built up again.

Like the rest of the Kremlin, the Holy Antechamber has been remodeled many times. Its current look dates from the middle of the 19th century when the Grand Kremlin Palace was built and connected to the Holy Antechamber by two new doorways. When it was first constructed, however, the antechamber was part of an ambitious building scheme in a very different style.

The white stone doorways inside the Holy Antechamber are covered with gold decoration.

ITALY COMES TO MOSCOW

THE HOLY ANTECHAMBER began as a grand entrance to the throne room in the upper story of the Palace of Facets, the oldest surviving palace in the Kremlin. The palace, often called the Faceted Hall, was built between 1487 and 1491 under the

The doorway between the Holy Antechamber and the Faceted Hall is even more elaborate on the hall side.

direction of two Italian architects who designed it in a style popular in Italy at the time.

Essentially a cube, with carved white limestone covering its front facade, the building now looks very plain beside the brightly colored onion-dome roofs of the buildings around it. At the time it was built, however, it was a flamboyant statement of the ambitions of Grand Duke Ivan III, known as Ivan the Great.

The Italian architects probably arrived in Moscow in the large entourage of Zoe Sophia Paleologus, Ivan's second wife and niece of the last emperor of Byzantium, which had followed the Roman Empire. Sophia was clever, ambitious—and large. She was said to weigh 160 kilograms (350 pounds).

She and Ivan suited each other. They both had bold dreams of making Russia the successor to the Byzantine Empire. Ivan even adopted the double-headed eagle, symbol of Byzantium, as his own symbol and the symbol of Russia. Rebuilding the Kremlin in the latest European fashion was his way of announcing his intention of making Russia a European power.

If the outside of the Palace of Facets looks plain, the inside is spectacular. The throne room, entered through the Holy

The walls of the Holy Antechamber and the Faceted Hall are covered with biblical scenes painted directly on the plaster. The current paintings were created in 1881.

Antechamber, takes up the entire upper floor of the palace, its roof supported by a single massive pillar in the center of the room. Today, murals cover the walls and ceiling, with gold trim and gold backgrounds. Four immense bronze chandeliers, made in the 19th century, hang from the ceiling. In Ivan III's day, the room looked different, but no less impressive.

Ivan the Terrible started his reign as a strong and successful leader, but ended it in madness.

Ivan probably walked through the Holy Antechamber into that grand room many times during his reign—to hold court, to meet with foreign delegations, and to hear petitions from his subjects. Sophia, however, would not have gone with him. According to Russian tradition, women weren't allowed at formal ceremonies. Sophia would have had to watch everything from a concealed alcove that the architects included in the Faceted Hall especially for that purpose.

THE TSAR THROWS A PARTY

TODAY, IMPORTANT STATE banquets are held in the Faceted Hall. Princes, presidents, priests, and prime ministers have been entertained there in the past few years.

But no modern banquet comes close to the feast held by Ivan III's grandson in 1552. Tsar Ivan IV, known as Ivan the Terrible, was just 22 when he won a great military victory. Upon returning to Moscow, he decided to celebrate.

He invited everyone involved to the victory banquet. They all filed through the Holy Antechamber into the Faceted Hall—the clergy whose prayers Ivan believed had helped win the day, officers of state, military men, and common soldiers who had fought bravely. The feasting lasted for three days.

Ambassadors coming to meet the tsar were first greeted in the Holy Antechamber. Gifts were unwrapped and placed on pillows for presentation to the tsar.

During the feast, Ivan read from an honor roll that detailed the exploits of the heroes, and presented them with gifts. He gave away horses, suits of armor, silver and gold goblets, fur-trimmed robes, money, land, and jobs. One report said the silver gifts alone weighed seven tons.

A chronicler wrote of the banquet: "No man had ever seen such splendor, so much celebration and merriment and generosity in the Kremlin Palace."

However, merriment and generosity were rare in Ivan's reign. He was notorious for irrational violence, and in his later years was clearly mad. People entered through the Holy Antechamber in anxiety and sometimes left in terror, especially if they had somehow provoked the tsar's anger. Ivan sat on his ivory throne, while his courtiers huddled against the walls, forbidden to advance unless he called them.

Generally it was safer not to be called.

Master Chancellor meets the tsar

In Ivan IV's court, it was safer to be a foreigner than a Russian. Like his grandfather, Ivan had great ambitions for Russia. Western European nations were sending ambassadors to Russia, and Ivan wanted to make sure they were impressed.

Richard Chancellor was certainly impressed. An English shipmaster in search of new trade routes for a group of English investors, Chancellor and his crew reached the north coast of Russia in the winter of 1553–54. Tsar Ivan heard of his arrival and invited him to Moscow.

After a long, cold journey by sled and a wait of 12 days in a house in Moscow, Chancellor and his companions were finally summoned to the palace. In the outer room, likely the Holy Antechamber, 100 courtiers sat, all dressed in cloth of gold from head to ankle. In the throne room itself, they found the tsar: "…on his head a diadem, or crown of gold, appareled with a robe all of goldsmith's work, and in his hand he held a scepter garnished, and beset with precious stones." Another 150 courtiers, also dressed in cloth of gold, were seated around the sides of the room.

Chancellor presented letters from England's King Edward VI, answered a few questions, and then the Englishmen were dismissed. A few hours later, they attended a royal banquet. Chancellor reported that even the servants wore cloth of gold and the tables were covered with so many gold dishes there was scarcely room for food.

"What shall I further say?" Chancellor wrote. "I never heard nor saw men so sumptuous."

TROUBLE WITH A BLACK CAT

THE FACETED HALL WAS USED for formal meetings as well as royal audiences. The boyar duma, an advisory council of nobles, met there. When a session of the duma was called, all the nobles passed through the Holy Antechamber and the gilded doorway into the great hall.

At the beginning of the 17th century, Russia was ruled by Prince Vasilii Shuisky, who had seized power unlawfully. Many of the nobles disliked the prince. He was ambitious and very superstitious, with a particular fear of black cats.

One day in 1606, Shuisky was in a meeting of the boyar duma when a huge black cat suddenly appeared. It might have sneaked through the door or been smuggled in by someone with no love for the prince. Standing in the middle of the hall, the cat mewed loudly.

Shuisky leaped up from the throne and dashed through the door to the Holy Antechamber, crossing himself. He was also reportedly reciting a prayer to St. Nicholas the Miracle Worker.

The duma was over for the day.

The nightmare of Peter the Great

FOR A FEW DECADES the nation was more stable, but by 1682, Russia was in trouble again. Fyodor III had died without having children, and two boys were possible heirs to the throne: Fyodor's invalid brother, Ivan, and Ivan's half-brother, 10-year-old Peter Romanov. Different groups chose sides, and on May 10 the feuding turned to violence.

A large crowd opposed to Peter and his mother's family gathered in the square in front of the royal palace, where the Grand Kremlin Palace is today, and the Palace of Facets. Members of Russia's elite guards were part of the crowd, their pikes—long poles with pointed metal tips—at the ready. More guards marched into the palace and hauled Peter's supporters, along with Peter and his mother, onto the Red Porch.

The Red Porch was an open gallery running along the outside of the royal palace's second story, combined with a wide staircase that connected it to the square below. At the top of the staircase was the Holy Antechamber, the entry into both palaces.

An officer ran up the staircase waving a list of people the mob wanted killed. As he read out the names, other guards seized 25 people and threw them off the porch onto the pikes below. Peter was forced to watch as his uncles, cousins, and friends were hacked to pieces on the stones. Then soldiers stormed through the Holy Antechamber and scoured the palaces for more victims.

The rampage lasted for four days and another 50 people were murdered, although the guards stopped short of attacking

This famous statue of Peter the Great as a bold horseman honors the man who had stood as a terrified boy on the Red Porch.

the royal family itself, including Peter and his mother. The mob drank all the wine in the tsar's cellar as well as some found in a nearby cathedral before the violence subsided.

Afterward, Peter and his brother were installed as joint tsars, with his sister acting as regent. Eventually, after his brother's death, Peter became the sole ruler and one of Russia's most famous tsars, known as Peter the Great. However, his experience that night on the Red Porch outside the Holy Antechamber never left him. He developed a nervous tremor that stayed with him all his life and nightmares that still caused him to wake up screaming 30 years later.

Peter also developed a lasting dislike of the Kremlin. Much later in his reign, he had a new palace built in St. Petersburg and moved the capital there.

THE END OF AN ERA

ALTHOUGH THE COURT MOVED to St. Petersburg, the Kremlin remained the location of most great state ceremonies, such as coronations and marriages, and the Holy Antechamber still played a role.

In the 1840s, the Grand Kremlin Palace was built next to the Palace of Facets. It incorporated the remains of several older

The staircase along the side of the Palace of Facets is called the Red Porch. It leads up to the Holy Antechamber.

palaces and churches, including the royal palace where Peter had lived as a child. The Holy Antechamber opened into the Faceted Hall on one side, but on the other side it now opened into the equally extravagant St. Vladimir's Hall in the Grand Kremlin Palace.

By long tradition, the tsars walked to their coronations through the Holy Antechamber and down the formal outside staircase of the Red Porch to the nearby Cathedral of the Assumption. The last coronation procession to pass through the Holy Antechamber was that of the last Tsar of Russia, Nicholas II, in 1896.

Tsar Nicholas II and Tsarina Alexandra Feodorovna stand on the Red Porch during their coronation in 1896.

In 1812, Napoleon's French army captured Moscow and occupied the Kremlin. Just a day later, a fire started in the city and wind spread the flames until much of the city was ablaze. Napoleon is said to have stood on the Red Porch and watched as the fire raged out of control and the city burned.

Just over a decade later, a series of revolutions rocked Russia and the era of the tsars came to a violent end.

THE KREMLIN IN THE DOLDRUMS

WHEN THE REVOLUTIONARY SMOKE began to clear in 1918, the new Communist government of Russia—later to become the Soviet Union—made Moscow its capital and the Kremlin its headquarters. However, the Communist leaders had no interest in preserving or using the tsar's gilded buildings, part of what they viewed as an old, corrupt world.

Under Vladimir Lenin, the first Communist leader of the new Russia, the Kremlin's buildings were merely neglected. When Josef Stalin became the next leader, many were torn down, including several churches and the Red Porch. The rest languished, unrepaired and unmaintained. From 1924 until after the death of Stalin in 1953, the Kremlin was closed to the public.

In 1955, people were invited into the Kremlin to see its art collections, museums, and historic buildings. In 1956, its first full year of operation as a museum, more than 800,000 people visited. Today, millions visit every year.

Tsar Nicholas II after his 1917 abdication. In July 1918, he was executed, along with all his family.

Powerful modern leaders—here, a former Russian president and two senior priests—enter the Faceted Hall through the Holy Antechamber.

Gradually, the government is restoring the old buildings. The Grand Kremlin Palace, the Holy Antechamber, and the Faceted Hall have all been restored to their 19th-century glory. In 1996, the grand staircase of the Red Porch was rebuilt.

POWER RETURNS TO THE HOLY ANTECHAMBER

MANY OF THE KREMLIN'S BUILDINGS are museums, but the Grand Kremlin Palace, the Holy Antechamber, and the Faceted Hall all make up part of the official residence of the President of the Russian Federation.

The Faceted Hall is now the president's official ceremonial hall.

In 1987, British Prime Minister Margaret Thatcher passed through the Holy Antechamber on her way to a banquet with Soviet leader Mikhail Gorbachev. Although the atmosphere was stiffly polite, both leaders gave speeches that made it clear they disagreed about many things.

A year later, the banquet guest walking through the Holy Antechamber was American President Ronald Reagan, fresh from friendlier talks with Gorbachev that helped wind down the Cold War, the decades-long antagonism between Western nations and the Russian-led Soviet Union.

Today, world rulers, religious leaders,

Josef Stalin rule Russia and the Soviet Union from the late 1920s until his death in 1953. The Red Porch was torn down during Stalin's time and rebuil in the 1990s.

Officers of the Moscow Kremlin Horse Guards prepare to review their troops at the base of the rebuilt Red Porch.

and less exalted guests pass arm in arm through the doors of the Holy Antechamber, where Vasilii Shuisky once fled from a cat, and feast in friendship in the great hall where Ivan the Terrible once ruled with absolute power.

DOOR OF NO RETURN:
Cape Coast Castle, Ghana

Like many slave forts on the Gold Coast of Africa—and there were dozens of them—Cape Coast Castle has a "door of no return." It's the castle's sole seaward door, a gateway to the stony beach where, day and night, waves roll in from the open Atlantic and crash on the shallow shore.

FOR MORE THAN THREE CENTURIES, cargo leaving the fort passed through that door. And for much of the fort's history, that cargo was human—thousands upon thousands of African people carried away to slavery in the Americas. For them, it was truly the door of no return.

Ironically, it was also a door of no return for many of the European traders, soldiers, workmen, and missionaries who arrived to seek their fortunes in the fort. Although they had the option of returning home, unlike the slaves, many died in Africa. Others stayed by choice, married locally, and raised families in the town near the castle.

The door, and the castle itself, have been repaired and rebuilt

The dark archway leads to the sea gate of Cape Coast Castle, the door of no return for many thousands of people.

many times over the centuries. Despite all the misery associated with it, Cape Coast Castle has been in business—of one kind or another—since 1653. And it's still in business. Today, it's one of Ghana's best-known museums.

BEACHFRONT PROPERTY IN EFUTU

THE FIRST PERSON to step through the castle's door from the seaward side may well have been a Polish trader who was working for a Swedish company that was renting space from an African king. Global trade came to the Gold Coast hundreds of years ago.

The Gold Coast is a long stretch of golden sand on the south-facing shoreline of Ghana, pounded by surf and punctuated here and there by low outcrops of rock. In the 17th century, the land was covered by thick tropical forest so lush that its fragrance drifted over the surf to European ships offshore.

Europeans were first drawn to the area by the gold that earned it the nickname of Gold Coast. The inland mines and rivers were famously rich in the precious metal. For centuries, the gold had been transported across the Sahara to Egypt and on to Europe. In England, gold coins were called guineas because the gold came from Guinea, another name for the Gold Coast.

Ship travel was faster, cheaper, and easier to control than the caravan trade, so by the 1650s half the nations of Europe

Cape Coast Castle sits on a rocky outcrop, one of the few along this part of Ghana's coast.

Today, DNA analysis is helping descendants of the slaves to find out where their ancestors came from and who they might be related to in modern Africa.

seemed to be jostling for space and trading rights along the Gold Coast. Traders and entrepreneurs arrived from Portugal, the Netherlands, Denmark, Sweden, Spain, France, Germany, and England.

In 1652, a Swedish company rented a rocky outcrop on the coast from the king of a small coastal kingdom called Efutu. Henrik Carlof, a Polish trader, arranged the deal. He supervised the building of the first door of no return in a small mud-brick fort christened Carlusborg.

Over the next few years, the fort passed through the hands of several nations. Finally, in 1664, an English fleet captured Carlusborg with help from the Danes and the army of Efutu. Carlusborg, soon renamed Cape Coast Castle, remained in British hands from then until 1957, when Ghana became an independent nation.

HUMAN GOLD ON THE SHORE

BY THE TIME THE ENGLISH walked in through the door of Cape Coast Castle, the big business was in slaves. For almost 250 years, the castle was the center of Britain's large and profitable slave trade. More than 11 million slaves were exported from trading posts on the west coast of Africa, and many thousands passed through Cape Coast Castle.

African slaves were in huge demand in the new European colonies in South America, the Caribbean, and parts of North America. European workers were not used to such heat and humidity, and had no immunity to tropical diseases. Africans, the plantation owners discovered, could work much longer and harder in the sun than Europeans and were less likely to sicken and die.

And they were cheap. Slaves received no wages and could not leave. Their labor made it possible for goods such as sugar, coffee, tobacco, and cotton to be sold around the world at prices that ordinary people could afford.

An 1821 engraving shows a group of slaves, chained at the neck, being taken from the African interior to a slave port on the coast.

As he waits, trapped on a bench, this slave seems without hope in this 19th-century engraving.

But the price of those goods was paid, many times over, by the suffering of the slaves.

THE NAMELESS ONES

FROM THE DATE OF THE CASTLE'S founding until 1807, when Britain abolished the slave trade in its territories, most of the people who walked through the door of no return were slaves—men, women, and children who had been taken by force from family and friends, deprived even of their names. They were listed in the castle's detailed ledgers only by gender and price: "a man slave £17/17/0" or "a girl 4ft 2½ inches £15/5/0."

Slavery, as a kind of domestic servitude, had a long tradition in northern and central Africa. Some slaves were prisoners of war, some owed debts, some were criminals, and some were simply kidnapped by slave traders.

For centuries, a few slaves had been exported from Africa as servants, mainly across the Sahara to the Mediterranean region. However, when Europeans established colonies in the Americas and began shipping slaves across the Atlantic, the slave trade changed. The number of slaves sent out

In the early 1800s, Elizabeth Dalzel, daughter of an African woman and the governor of Cape Coast Castle, started a newspaper campaign that led to the liberation of white Christian slaves being held in North Africa.

of Africa exploded and their treatment, both by slave traders and by their owners in the New World, grew more and more cruel.

Most of the people who were shipped out of Cape Coast Castle as slaves came from inland, up to 300 kilometers (200 miles) from the coast. They were captured or purchased by African slave traders, chained, marched down forest paths to the coast, and sold to European and American buyers who congregated at the castles.

Because of the shallow coast and dangerous surf, the slave ships had to stay offshore in safer waters called the roads. Traders came ashore in local surf boats, just like the boats still used by fishermen along the coast of Ghana. A ship might spend months in the roads while the slave trader bought enough people for a full cargo.

Some of the slaves would be herded through the door of no return immediately, loaded on surf boats, and stowed below decks on a slave ship until the rest of the space was filled. Others were kept in the castle's dungeons, called slave holes, until the ship was ready to sail. Then they too were bundled through the door to waiting surf boats and onto ships bound for Brazil, Jamaica, Barbados, Virginia, or other colonies in the Americas.

Every stage of the journey was dangerous. People died on the long walk to the coast, in the slave holes, in the sea if a surf boat capsized, and in the holds of ships. Even if they survived all those dangers, they faced a lifetime of slavery in a distant land—with no return, ever, to their homes and families.

This is the view slaves saw as they staggered up the ramp from their underground prison, on their way to the door of no return.

FROM HOSTAGE TO PRIEST

NOT EVERY AFRICAN who passed through the door of no return was a slave bound for overseas plantations. Some were merchants and tradespeople who loaded cargo, bought and sold goods, or performed specialized jobs such as operating surf boats.

For a few, including Kwekwi, passing through the door led to a completely different life.

In 1753, the British signed an important treaty with the Fante people, who had become the owners of the land where Cape Coast Castle stood. As part of the treaty, the Fante leaders handed over four boys as pledges of their good intent. One of them was Kwekwi.

Kwekwi went through the door of no return, but as a hostage, not a slave. The British sent him to London and put him in the care of a priest. Kwekwi spent 11 years in London. He was a clever boy. He learned English, attended school, and eventually became a priest in the Church of England.

In 1765, he returned to Cape Coast Castle as Reverend Philip Quaque, the newly appointed chaplain of the castle. Quaque was accompanied by his English wife and her attendant. However, the marriage didn't last long. Both women died within months, victims of tropical diseases.

Quaque survived, married a local woman, and had a number of children. He served as chaplain of Cape Coast Castle for decades, and eventually witnessed the abolition of the slave trade. Philip Quaque, or Kwekwi, died in 1817, more than 60 years after his relatives had given him to the British to be sent through the door of no return.

SURVIVING THE SEASONING

THE FATE OF REVEREND QUAQUE'S first wife and her companion was far from unusual. Many of the British who came through Cape Coast Castle's door died within weeks or months. Their first year in Africa was called "seasoning." If they survived their seasoning, the European residents were considered to have a chance of returning home.

Just getting ashore through the surf was the first challenge. Newcomers staggered in, soaked to the skin after wading

Below the castle walls, where surf boats once carried cargo and slaves, local fishing boats now gather.

In 1877, when the British moved their colonial headquarters out of Cape Coast Castle, they looked back over temperature records and discovered it was the hottest place on the Gold Coast.

through crashing waves. Even the officers and women, who were carried ashore by boatmen or cargo handlers, were generally wet through. If a boat capsized, passengers often drowned.

Once they reached the castle, dangers multiplied. The tropical climate offered viruses, parasites, and other illnesses the Europeans had never been exposed to. Newcomers died from malaria, yellow fever, and dysentery. They suffered from the heat, drank contaminated water or liquor, and endured medical remedies that did more harm than good. To make matters worse, occasional epidemics of diseases such as smallpox swept through the castle.

In 1769, 48 soldiers were sent to Cape Coast Castle in February. By the end of May, 40 were dead.

Surviving the seasoning year was no guarantee of safety. An alarming number of people still died, and those who survived were often ill. In August 1801, for example, two-thirds of the officers in the castle were sick. Of all the British men and women who came to Cape Coast Castle in search of adventure or fortune, few survived the experience unscarred in mind or body. Many didn't survive at all.

THE END OF THE TRADE

SLAVES WERE STILL A VALUABLE commodity in 1807, but the slave trade itself had lost support in Britain. A long campaign succeeded in persuading Parliament to abolish the trade within all British territories and by all British subjects, even though most slave-trading nations continued the practice for decades longer.

The slave traders of Cape Coast Castle were naturally unhappy about the change in law, since it made 90 percent of their trade illegal. In the last few weeks before the law took effect, frantic trading took place.

Ironically, one of the biggest customers for slaves in the final days was the British government itself. With most of its troops engaged in European wars, Britain was short of soldiers to guard its Caribbean colonies. It solved the problem by buying hundreds of young men to serve in its West India Regiment.

Letters show that the British government delayed abolition just long

This stone slide might have been used to deliver food or water to slaves held in the slave hole.

Big guns still line the walls of Cape Coast Castle, rusting in the salt and humidity.

enough for the army to make one last purchase. In the spring of 1807, hundreds of boys and young men were led in chains out the door of no return to be shipped to the West Indies and enrolled as slave soldiers. Their job: to defend the Caribbean colonies from both invaders and slave revolts.

Even more ironically, some of the young soldiers returned. In 1819, after the war in Europe ended, the West India Regiment was sent to West Africa to defend the growing British possessions there. In 1821, part of the regiment was stationed on the Gold Coast—almost certainly including slave soldiers who had been shipped from Cape Coast Castle's door of no return less than 15 years earlier.

THE LADY ADVENTURER

THE SLAVE TRADE ENDED IN 1807, but Cape Coast Castle continued to serve British interests in Africa. The government encouraged the development of palm plantations. Soon, casks of palm oil were the chief cargo hauled through the door to waiting surf boats. The castle also became a base for missionaries bringing Christianity to West Africa and for the development of British colonies in the region.

In 1821, the British government took over ownership of the castle from the merchant company that had run it during the slave era. What had begun as a bit of beachfront leased from the king of Efutu by Sweden became an important component of the British Empire.

One of the more unusual people to enter through the door of no return during this era was a writer, Letitia Elizabeth Landon. She wrote popular romantic stories featuring exotic locations, doomed women, and faithless men.

In 1838, Landon married George Maclean, governor of Cape Coast Castle. Stepping through the castle door a few weeks later, Landon appeared to be thrilled with her new life as she explored the castle and countryside. But something was wrong. Less than two months after she arrived, Letitia Landon was found dead in her room. She had apparently killed herself by drinking poison, but suicide was considered shameful in those days and her death was ruled accidental. Even with the slave trade gone, death and loss still hung about the door of Cape Coast Castle.

THE CASTLE TODAY

TODAY, CAPE COAST CASTLE is a museum, owned by the independent nation of Ghana, and the door of no return is a wide archway through the castle wall to the beach where local fishermen land their catch.

Tour guides lead columns of schoolchildren and parties of tourists around the castle, into its slave holes, past the graves of Letitia Elizabeth Landon and her husband, George Maclean—and through the archway. On its seaward side is a new inscription, added in 1998: "Door of Return."

Many of the tourists are descendants of people shipped as slaves from West Africa, perhaps through that very door. For them, the door of no return has been transformed into a "door of return"—a homecoming to the land of their ancestors and a chance to reclaim their stolen heritage.

Cape Coast Castle today is the backdrop to a busy market scene in the town of Cape Coast.

DOOR TO HEAVEN:
The Meridian Gate, Beijing

The Meridian Gate, or Wu Men, is the south gate of the Forbidden City in Beijing, home of the emperors of China, who were also known as the Sons of Heaven.

TODAY, THE FORBIDDEN CITY is a vast museum, and thousands of visitors—Chinese and foreigners alike—stream through the Meridian Gate every day. But for almost six centuries, the Meridian Gate was as close as ordinary citizens of China ever came to their emperor, and closer than some of them wished to come.

The word "gate" is a bit misleading. The Meridian Gate is as high as an eight-story building and designed to intimidate, not to welcome. It has a central section and two side wings, laid out like three sides of a square. The Meridian Gate squats in the center of the southern wall of the Forbidden City, with its back to the emperor's palaces and its arms reaching south, completely dominating the large, stone-paved plaza between them.

Three square entrances pierce the flat, brick-red, concrete wall of the gate's central section. Only the emperor used the main entrance, higher than a two-story building. Members of the imperial family entered through the smaller western gateway, and civil and military officials with the proper credentials came in through the eastern entrance.

Only the emperor was allowed to enter the large central opening in the Meridian Gate.

FRONT YARD OF THE SON OF HEAVEN

ON THE OTHER SIDE of the Meridian Gate, the inward side that few people ever saw, the three entrances open onto a vast courtyard. A canal called the Golden Stream winds gently across the courtyard, and five white stone bridges lead straight north to another large gate, the Gate of Supreme Harmony. Directly north of that gate are three large raised halls: the Hall of Supreme Harmony, the Hall of Central Harmony, and the northernmost Hall of Preserving Harmony.

Modern soldiers stand guard outside the Meridian Gate, but not to prevent ordinary people from going inside.

These were the public areas of the Forbidden City, the places where the emperor met officials and ambassadors. During the early 18th century, all civil and military officials were required to report to the Forbidden City three times a month, before dawn. They passed through the gate and lined up in that huge courtyard to pay homage to their ruler. It was a constant reminder of the emperor's power over their lives.

The public areas were all that most officials, even senior officials, ever saw of the Forbidden City. The private quarters of the imperial family and its servants were at the northern end of the Forbidden City, behind even more gates. They weren't family quarters in any way we would understand today. According to court documents, Emperor Wanli, an extravagant man who ruled in the late 16th century, had tens of thousands of servants, officials, and courtiers in his household, many of whom lived within the Forbidden City.

The whole massive complex, said to have a total of 9999 rooms, was built in just 14 years at the beginning of the 15th century, after a Ming dynasty emperor decided to move his capital from Nanjing to Beijing. Although bits of the Forbidden City have been repaired and rebuilt over the years, it still looks much the same as it did when it was completed in 1421.

THE FIRST EMPEROR OF THE FORBIDDEN CITY

EMPEROR YONGLE WAS THE FIRST of many Chinese rulers to pass through the central arch of the Meridian Gate. He was the son of the first Ming emperor, who had been a peasant, a

Inside the Forbidden City, the Golden Stream winds across the square behind the Meridian Gate.

A gilded bronze lion guards one of the palaces within the Forbidden City.

Buddhist monk, and a rebel before he seized control of China and declared himself emperor.

Unlike his father, Emperor Yongle had been raised in the imperial court and exposed to courtly intrigue. He was powerful, ruthless, and very successful.

During much of the Ming dynasty, which lasted from 1368 to 1644, China was the wealthiest, most sophisticated country in the world. Emperor Yongle could afford military campaigns against the troublesome Mongol tribes in the north—and he could afford the massive building project of the Forbidden City. He could even afford to send the famous admiral, Zheng He, and his fleet as far as the shores of India, Arabia, and Africa—not to trade or acquire new territory, but to show those distant lands the wealth and might of China.

To adorn his beautiful new palace in Beijing, the emperor ordered works of art created, part of the huge collection that visitors to the Forbidden City enjoy today. And he commissioned the largest encyclopedia in history, made up of 12,000 volumes and written by 2000 scholars.

MERIDIAN GATE IN THE LAST DAYS OF THE MING

THE EXTRAVAGANT EMPEROR WANLI came to the throne in 1572, at the age of nine. He reigned for 48 years during the dying days of the Ming dynasty, 150 years after the death of Emperor Yongle.

By the beginning of Emperor Wanli's reign, the role of the emperor had changed. Emperor Yongle had led five military campaigns against the Mongols, and his war lance was preserved in a tower on top of the Meridian Gate. Emperor Wanli, even as an adult, seldom ventured beyond the Forbidden City and left most of the governing to his officials.

However, even if he rarely passed through the central arch, the Meridian Gate played an important and sometimes bloody role in the emperor's exercise of power.

From the emperor's balcony, the people in the square outside the Meridian Gate appear tiny.

Today the Forbidden City preserves more than a million individual artifacts. They include the elaborately decorated Dragon Throne from which the emperor issued decrees and the bicycle treasured by the last emperor, Puyi.

One of the most important ceremonies held at the Meridian Gate was the disposal of prisoners of war. The emperor sat on a balcony above the imperial entryway, looking out over the great square hemmed in by the gate's two wings. Senior military officers stood on either side of him, and beside them stood long lines of imperial guards in shiny armor and helmets with red tassels.

Below in the huge courtyard, thousands of court officials and soldiers watched as chained prisoners of war were led into the courtyard to face the emperor. The prisoners were forced to kneel on the granite paving stones while the minister of justice read out a list of their crimes. Then the minister asked the emperor to order the prisoners to be executed in the marketplace.

The emperor's ritual response was, "Take them there; be it so ordered." The two nobles beside the emperor repeated the words. Then they were repeated by four guardsmen, then by eight, and so on—until the whole glittering battalion was shouting the order for the prisoners' deaths, and the thousands of people in the square had no doubt about the power of this emperor.

CONTROLLING THE GOVERNMENT

OFFICIALS IN THE LATE YEARS of the Ming dynasty had a great deal of power, but at great risk. The punishment for displeasing the emperor was severe. The worst punishments were meted out at the Meridian Gate.

In 1577, when he was still in his teens, Emperor Wanli punished four senior officials who tried to tell him that his first grand-secretary was corrupt. (It was true!) They were stripped of their robes before the Meridian Gate and beaten with whipping sticks—jointed wooden clubs that caused serious injury.

The emperor once sat on this balcony to review his troops or decide the fate of prisoners of war.

Emperor Wanli handed out that kind of punishment more than once. After the beating, an official's name would be removed from the civil service register, resulting in poverty and disgrace for him and his family.

Soldiers dragged the beaten and humiliated men through the Meridian Gate and dumped them outside the square, where their families were allowed to collect them. If anyone other than a family member helped the victims, the helper was likely to find himself at the wrong end of a whipping stick too.

During China's imperial days, only the most senior officials were allowed through the Meridian Gate, and even they had to get down from their horses or chairs at the gate and walk the rest of the way into the Forbidden City.

BUREAUCRACY IN A GATE

NOT ALL THE BUSINESS at the Meridian Gate led to the spilling of blood. One of its important functions was to connect the imperial government and the people.

The gate's two huge wings contained the Office of the Supervising Secretaries. All official documents were sent to the Office, where scores of scribes busily created copies.

Once a document reached the hands of the Supervising Secretaries, it officially became public. There are stories of people who got in terrible trouble because their private notes were accidentally delivered to the Meridian

Gate and became official documents. No matter how personal or petty the note, it was a serious offence to remove it from the Meridian Gate offices.

Among the public documents were records of conversations between the emperor and his senior officials. The senior official would dutifully make notes and deliver them to the Meridian Gate. Once they were copied and published, the emperor's remarks became official imperial policy.

THE HONOR OF THE EMPEROR'S PORTAL

IN 1644, THE LAST DYNASTY of imperial China, the Qing Dynasty, took control of the country. The Qing emperors moved into the Forbidden City and adopted the privileges of the Ming emperors—including the emperor's exclusive right to use the central portal of the Meridian Gate.

Traditionally, however, there were two exceptions to this rule. The first allowed a woman to enter through the magnificent gate.

Like the Ming before them, the Qing emperors considered the use of the emperor's entrance into the Forbidden City the highest honor that could be bestowed. It was an honor given to the emperor's bride one time only, on her wedding day.

According to tradition, the bride chosen for the emperor stayed in her father's house in the city until the wedding day. She rose just past midnight on her wedding day to begin preparing for the great occasion. Ladies from the royal court helped her dress in layers of silk robes, embroidered and decorated with jewels.

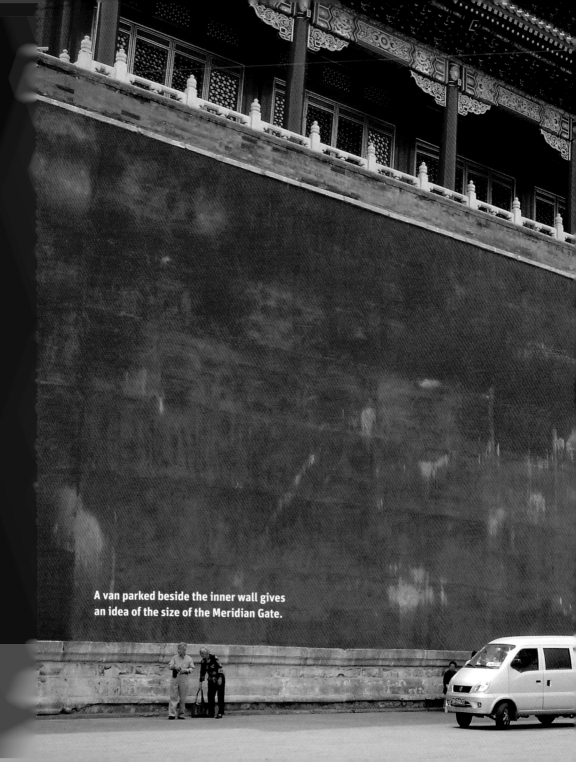

A van parked beside the inner wall gives
an idea of the size of the Meridian Gate.

> **The Meridian Gate, or Wu Men, is also known as Wu Feng Lou, meaning Five Phoenixes Tower.**

They arranged on her head a red silk headdress studded, according to one 19th-century newspaper report, with pearls, coral, rubies, amethysts, jasper, a variety of other precious stones, and blue feathers. Strings of coral beads were draped around her neck and jeweled earrings hung from her ears.

Before dawn, a special enclosed chair supported by poles, with silk upholstery and silver phoenixes on the corners of its roof, arrived to collect her. Her path lit by 60 lantern-bearers, the bride was carried through the dark streets of Beijing and through the central arch of every gate into the Forbidden City, including the emperor's exclusive arch through the Meridian Gate.

At last, deep within the Forbidden City, the porters delivered her to the wedding chamber, called the Palace of Earthly Tranquility. There, the emperor removed his bride's veil and the couple saw one another's faces for the first time.

SCHOLARSHIP PAYS

THE ONLY OTHER PEOPLE permitted to pass through the emperor's arch in the Meridian Gate were the winners of a scholastic competition. China had traditionally valued scholarship, and such a vast empire needed many well-educated, competent officials.

Every three years, scholars who had passed local and

national examinations gathered in the Forbidden City to be tested on a series of topics chosen by the emperor himself. Early in the morning, the scholars entered through the side archways of the Meridian Gate and lined up in the huge terrace within the Forbidden City. They made the full kowtow, the traditional mark of respect made by everyone in the presence of the emperor. It involved kneeling and hitting their heads on the stones of the terrace nine times.

Then the emperor would emerge and take part in examining

Emperor Teaon-Kwang reviews his guards before the Meridian Gate in the first part of the 19th century.

Modern tourists casually come and go through the great gate.

the scholars. Most had studied for years for this moment. To score well in the emperor's examination would assure them of good jobs for life, with wealth and respect for their families and themselves.

The top three scholars in each set of examinations received a special honor. They were given the right, just once, to leave the city through the central portal of the Meridian Gate.

THE END OF EMPIRE

OVER THE SIX CENTURIES of the Ming and Qing dynasties, 24 emperors—among them, scholars, statesmen, artists, warriors, and a few madmen—stepped through the central arch of the Meridian Gate. But China and the world were changing, and the days of imperial rule were coming to an end.

The last emperor to pass through the Meridian Gate, Emperor Xuantong, arrived in 1908 as a toddler. In 1912, just after his sixth birthday, a revolution overthrew the empire and established a republic. The child-emperor abdicated, although he and his family were allowed to live in comfort in the private quarters of the Forbidden City for several more years.

Parts of the Forbidden City were opened to the public as a

museum. Suddenly, people could walk through the Meridian Gate instead of kneeling before it until the emperor summoned them. They could view the inner courtyard and magnificent buildings without fear of being beaten or executed for violating the imperial privacy. It was a shocking change.

Even more dramatic changes were on the way. In 1924, Emperor Xuantong, the last Chinese emperor, gave up all rights to the title and left the Forbidden City. He was now a young man of 18 and was called, simply, Puyi. Years of civil war and world war followed. Finally, in 1949, the Chinese Communist Party led by Mao Zedong took control of the country and created the People's Republic of China.

GLORY AND EXCESS

ODDLY ENOUGH, the home of the emperors of China has flourished in the People's Republic. The center of government has moved to new buildings in the heart of Beijing, and the Forbidden City is now officially the Palace Museum, preserved as a reminder of both the glory and the excesses of imperial China.

Emperor Xuantong (Puyi) stands beside his father, Prince Chun, who holds Puyi's younger brother.

The emperors of the past would never have imagined a crowd like this surging through the Meridian Gate's imperial central arch.

Exquisite treasures—paintings, pottery, elaborate clocks, and thrones inlaid with ivory and precious stones—collected by the emperors, often at the expense of their subjects, are on display for everyone to enjoy. And everyone does. The grounds and palaces, gardens and tranquil ponds, once the private preserve of the imperial family, are now popular destinations for both tourists and Chinese citizens.

And the Meridian Gate, including the emperor's central arch, is open to the world.

Further reading

Petra and the Nabataeans

Barnes, Trevor. *Archaeology*. Boston: Kingfisher, 2004.

Stefoff, Rebecca. *Finding the Lost Cities*. New York: Oxford University Press, 1998.

Taylor, Jane. *Petra and the Lost Kingdom of the Nabataeans*. Cambridge, MA: Harvard University Press, 2002.

Castel Sant'Angelo (Hadrian's Mausoleum)

Adams, Simon. *Castles and Forts*. Boston: Kingfisher, 2003.

Barghusen, Joan D. *Daily Life in Ancient and Modern Rome (Cities through Time)*. Minneapolis: Runestone Press, 1999.

Stewart, David. *Inside Ancient Rome*. New York: Enchanted Lion Books, 2005.

Spruce Tree House and the Ancestral Puebloans

Arnold, Caroline. *Ancient Cliff Dwellers of Mesa Verde*. Minneapolis: Tandem Library, 2001.

Crewe, Sabrina, and Dale Anderson. *The Anasazi Culture at Mesa Verde (Events That Shaped America)*. Strongsville, OH: Gareth Stevens, 2002.

Roberts, David. *In Search of the Old Ones*. New York: Simon & Schuster, 1996.

Sankoré Mosque, Islam, and Timbuktu

Brook, Larry. *Daily Life in Ancient and Modern Timbuktu*. Minneapolis: Runestone Press, Lerner, 1999.

Khan, Rukhsana. *Muslim Child*. Toronto: Napoleon, 1999.

McKissack, Patricia and Fredrick. *The Royal Kingdoms of Ghana, Mali, and Songhay: Life in Medieval Africa*. New York: Henry Holt, 1994.

Traitors' Gate and the Tower of London

Hynson, Colin. *The Tower of London (Place in History)*. Tunbridge Wells, UK: ticktock Media, 2006.

Parnell, Geoffrey. *The Tower of London, Past and Present*. Gloucestershire, UK: Sutton Publishing , 1998.

Riley, Gail Blasser. *Tower of London: England's Ghostly Castle (Castles, Palaces and Tombs)*. New York: Bearport Publishing, 2006.

The Holy Antechamber and the Kremlin

Greene, Meg. *The Russian Kremlin (Building History)*. Farmington Hills, MI: Lucent Books, 2001.

Price, Sean. *Ivan the Terrible: Tsar of Death (A Wicked History)*. London: Franklin Watts, 2008.

Shifman, Barry. *Gifts to the Tzars 1500–1700: Treasures from the Kremlin*. London: Abrams, 2001.

Cape Coast Castle and the Atlantic Slave Trade

Johnson, Charles. *Middle Passage* (novel). New York: Scribner, 1998.

St. Clair, William. *The Door of No Return: The History of Cape Coast Castle and the Atlantic Slave Trade*. New York: BlueBridge, 2007.

Sharp, S. Pearl, and Virginia Schomp. *The Slave Trade and the Middle Passage (The Drama of African-American History)*. New York: Benchmark Books, 2006.

The Meridian Gate and the Forbidden City

Knox, Barbara. *Forbidden City: China's Imperial Palace (Castles, Palaces and Tombs)*. New York: Bearport, 2006.

Marx, Trish. *Elephants and Golden Thrones: Inside China's Forbidden City*. New York: Abrams Books for Young Readers, 2008.

Morley, Jacqueline. *You Wouldn't Want To Be in the Forbidden City! A Sheltered Life You'd Rather Avoid*. London: Franklin Watts, 2008

Selected bibliography

Adams, Karen R. "Through the Looking Glass: The Environment of the Ancient Mesa Verdeans." In *The Mesa Verde World*, ed. David Grant Noble. Sante Fe, NM: SAR Press, 2006.

Alexandrov, Viktor. *The Kremlin: Nerve-Centre of Russian History*. Trans. by Roy Monkcom. London: George Allen & Unwin, 1963.

Billings, Malcolm. "Ghana's Slave Castles." *History Today*. August 1999.

Burckhardt, John. *Travels in Syria and the Holy Land by the late John Lewis Burckhardt*. London: Association for Promoting the Discovery of the Interior Parts of Africa, 1822.

Bury, J. B. *History of the Later Roman Empire*. London: Macmillan, 1923.

"China's Imperial Wedding." *The New York Times*. Apr. 30, 1889.

Davies, Penelope J. E. "The Phoenix and the Flames: Death, Rebirth and the Imperial Landscape of Rome." *Mortality*. Vol. 5, No. 3 (2000): 237–58.

de Villiers, Marq, and Sheila Hirtle. *Timbuktu: The Sahara's Fabled City of Gold*. New York: Walker, 2007.

Farajat, Suleiman, and Sami Al-Nawafleh. *Report on the al-Khazna Courtyard Excavation at Petra (2003 Season)*. Unpublished ms. Petra, Jordan: Petra Archaeology Park, 2004.

Freeman, Charles. "Hadrian's Hall." *History Today*. Vol. 57, No. 1 (Jan. 2007): 10–11.

Froissart, Jean. *Chronicles*. Selected, translated, and edited by Geoffrey Brereton. Baltimore, MD: Penguin, 1968. Originally completed circa 1400.

Ge, Liangyan. "Rou Putuan: Voyeurism, Exhibitionism, and the 'Examination Complex.'" *Chinese Literature: Essays, Articles, Reviews (CLEAR)*. Vol. 20 (Dec. 1998): 127–52.

Gendall, Graham. "Ghana's Golden Coast." *History Today*. Vol. 57, Issue 3 (Mar. 2007).

Hairston, Julia L. "Skirting the Issue: Machiavelli's Caterina Sforza." *Renaissance Quarterly*. Vol. 53, No. 3. (Autumn 2000): 687–712.

Hakluyt, Richard. *Voyages and Discoveries: The Principal Navigations, Voyages, Traffiques and Discoveries of the English Nation*. Edited, abridged and introduced by Jack Beeching. Harmondsworth, Middlesex, UK: Penguin, 1972. Originally published 1598–1600.

Hanbury-Tenison, Robin. *The Oxford Book of Exploration*. Oxford: Oxford University Press, 1994.

Holdsworth, May. *The Forbidden City*. Hong Kong: Oxford University Press, 1988.

Huang, Ray. *1587: A Year of No Significance: The Ming Dynasty in Decline*. New Haven and London: Yale University Press, 1981.

Joukowsky, Martha Sharp. "Portal to Petra." *Natural History*. Vol. 112, Issue 8 (Oct. 2003): 40–43.

Kemp, Renée. "An apology in Ghana." *Essence*. Oct. 1995, Vol. 26, Issue 6.

Lawler, Andrew. "Reconstructing Petra." *Smithsonian*. Vol. 38, Issue 3 (June 2007).

Leake, Harvey C. "The Wetherills, the Bureau of Ethnology and Mesa Verde: A Difference of Perspective." *The Archaeological Society of New Mexico* 33 (2007): 71–80.

Levtzion, Nehemia. *Ancient Ghana and Mali*. London: Methuen, 1973.

Libbey, William Jr. "Moscow, the Magnificent." *Journal of the American Geographical Society of New York*. Vol. 20. (1888): 273–94.

Llewellyn, Peter. *Rome in the Dark Ages*. London: Constable, 1996.

Majanlahti, Anthony. *The Families Who Made Rome*. London: Pimlico, 2006.

McKissack, Patricia and Fredrick. *The Royal Kingdoms of Ghana, Mali, and Songhay: Life in Medieval Africa*. New York: Henry Holt, 1994.

Mears, Kenneth J. *The Tower of London: 900 Years of English History*. Oxford: Phaidon Press, 1988.

Minnis, Paul E. "Prehistoric Diet in the Northern Southwest: Macroplant Remains from Four Corners Feces." *American Antiquity*. Vol. 54, No. 3. (July 1989): 543–63.

Murowchick, Robert E., general ed. *China: Ancient Culture, Modern Land*. Norman, OK: University of Oklahoma Press, 1994.

Myers, Jenny, and Sheila Petersen. "Seven Go To Timbuktu (29 January – 16 February 2007)." *Whispering Gallery*, Fall 2007: 13–16.

National Park Service. U.S. Department of the Interior. *Mesa Verde National Park*. http://www.nps.gov/meve.

Parnell, Geoffrey. *The Tower of London, Past & Present*. Gloucestershire, UK: Sutton, 1998.

Payne, Robert, and Nikita Romanoff. *Ivan the Terrible*. New York: Thomas Y. Crowell, 1975.

Perry, Megan A. "Life and Death in Nabataea: The North Ridge Tombs and Nabataean Burial Practices." *Near Eastern Archaeology*. Vol. 65, No. 4 (2002).

Pierce, S. Rowland. "The Mausoleum of Hadrian and the Pons Aelius." *The Journal of Roman Studies*. Vol. 15. (1925): 75–103.

Procopius. *History of the Wars*. English trans. H. B. Dewing. London: William Heinemann, 1919.

Rawski, Evelyn Sakakida. *The Last Emperors: A Social History of Qing Imperial Institutions*. Berkeley: University of California Press, 1998.

Roberts, David. "Riddles of the Anasazi." *Smithsonian*. Vol. 34, Issue 4 (July 2003).

———. *In Search of the Old Ones*. New York: Simon & Schuster, 1996.

Rodimzeva, Irina, Nikolai Rachmanov, and Alfons Raimann. *The Kremlin and Its Treasures*. New York: Rizzoli, 1987. Original Russian edition, 1986.

St. Clair, William. *The Door of No Return: The History of Cape Coast Castle and the Atlantic Slave Trade*. New York: BlueBridge, 2007.

Sidi, Ali Ould. "Monuments and Traditional Know-how: The Example of Mosques in Timbuktu." *Museum*. Vol. 58, No 1–2 (2006): 49–58.

Smith, Duane A. *Mesa Verde National Park: Shadows of the Centuries*. Boulder, CO: University Press of Colorado, 2002. Originally published in 1988 by the University Press of Kansas.

Stephen, Alexander M. "Hopi Tales." *The Journal of American Folklore*. Vol. 42, No. 163. (Jan. – Mar. 1929): 1–72.

Strabo. *Geography*. Eds. H. C. Hamilton, and W. Falconer, M. A. (1857). Available online at http://www.perseus.tufts.edu/cgi-bin/ptext?doc=Perseus%3Atext%3A1999.01.0239.

Taylor, Jane. *Petra and the Lost Kingdom of the Nabataeans*. Cambridge, MA: Harvard University Press, 2002.

Torres-Reyes, Ricardo. *Mesa Verde National Park: An Administrative History 1906–1970*. Washington, DC: U.S. Dept. of the Interior, 1970.

Waley-Cohen, Joanna. "Commemorating War in Eighteenth-Century China." *Modern Asian Studies*. Vol. 30, No. 4, *Special Issue: War in Modern China*. (Oct., 1996): 869–99.

Weir, Alison. *The Princes in the Tower*. New York: Ballantine Books, 1992.

"What's in a Name?" *Archaeology*. Vol 59, Issue 4 (July–Aug. 2006): 12.

Willard, James Field. "Inland Transportation in England during the Fourteenth Century." *Speculum*. Vol. 1 No. 4 (Oct. 1926): 361–74.

Wilson, Derek. *The Tower: The Tumultuous History of the Tower of London from 1078*. New York: Charles Scribner's Sons, 1979.

Index

Note: Page numbers in italics indicate illustrations.

Charles V (Holy Roman Emperor), 33, 35, 36
China, 21, 123, 128, 132, 133, 136, 138, 139
Chinese, 123, 126, 139, 141
Christian, 18, 19, 30, 113
Christianity, 121
Cliff Palace, 46
cliff, 5, 7, 8, 19, 22, 39, 41, 42, *43*, 44, 45, 46, 47, 49, 53, 54, 55
coffee, 111
Cold War, 105
colonies, 111, 113, 114, 119, 120, 121
Colosseum, 37
Communist, 102, 139
coprolites, 54
corn, 42, 44, 55
coronation, 80, 81, 82, 83, 86, 89, 100, 101
cotton, 111
court, 41, 86, 94, 96, 100, 126, 128, 130, 133
courtyard, 56, 60, 62, 66, 125, 126, 130, 139
crossbows, 29
Crusaders, 18
cypress trees, 25, 38

Dalzel, Elizabeth, 113
dams, 15, 19
Denmark, 110
desert, 5, 16, 57, 61, 66, 67, 69
Dio, 25–26
disease, 31, 111, 116, 118
drought, 54, 55
duma, 97
dynasty, 25, 31, 83, 126, 128, 129, 131, 133

earthquake, 19, 70
Edward I, 75, 79, 80
Edward II, 78, 79,
Edward IV, 81
Edward V, 81–82
Edward VI, 96
Edward Longshanks, 75
   See also Edward I
Efutu, 108, 110, 121
Egypt, 5, 13, 23, 61, 63, 109
Elizabeth I, 1, 83, 85, *85*, 86
emperor, 23, 25, 26, 33, 38, 93, 123, 124, 126, 128, 129, 130, 131, 132, 133, 136, 137, 138, 139, 141
empire, 16, 19, 23, 26, 64, 69, 93, 121, 136, 138
England, 1, 73, 74, 80, 82, 96, 109, 110, 116
English, 96, 110, 116
Europe, 18, 28, 33, 47, 61, 69, 109, 119
European, 19, 45, 69, 93, 96, 107, 109, 111, 113, 114, 117, 118, 119
examination, 137–138
executed, 73, 84, 85, 103, 130, 139

Faceted Hall, 89, 91, 92, 93, 94, 97, 101, *104*, 105. *See also* Palace of Facets
Fante, 116
feast, 16, 18, 94, 95, 106
Fewkes, Jesse Walter, 52–53
Fez, 63
fire, 42, 44, 54, 55, 88, 102
floods, 1, 7, 11, 15, *18*, 19, 59
Forbidden City, 123, 126–130, 132, 133, 136–139
forest, 46, 54, 69, 109, 114
fort, 4, 18, 36, 107, 110
fortifications, 38, 75

Photo credits

2, 88 © Jackie Meeks; 3 © istockphoto/fb1807016; 4 © istockphoto/Benjamin Porter; 6 © tkachuk/shutterstock.com; 7 © Clara Natoli/shutterstock.com; 9 © Marta Mirecka/shutterstock.com; 10 © Birute Vijeikiene/shutterstock.com; 12, 14, 15, 18, 22 © Petra National Trust; 17 © OPIS/shutterstock.com; 20 Public domain, courtesy of Petra National Trust; 24 istockphoto.com/fotoVoyager; 25 © plastique/shutterstock.com; 27 © Eugene Mogilnikov/shutterstock.com; 29, 38 © Diego Manzetti; 30 © Ronald Sumners/shutterstock.com; 32 © istockphoto.com/Marisa Allegra; 34 © Denis Babenko/shutterstock.com; 36 Public domain, courtesy of Diego Manzetti and Christine Palmer, www.romanbookshelf.com; 40, 41, 44, 45, 47, 49, 52, 54 © National Park Service; 43, 50-51, 90, 100, 115, 119, 122, 134-135, 138 © Galen Frysinger; 48 © National Park Service/Nordenskiöld photograph; 56 © Wendy Kaveney Photography/shutterstock.com; 58, 59 © Dan Heller; 60, 63 © istockphoto.com/Alan Tobey; 65 © ayazad/shutterstock.com; 66 © istockphoto.com/David Kerkhoff; 67 © Jeremy Meyer; 68 © Betty Moxon; 71 © istockphoto.com/Roberta Bianchi; 74 © Olive DePonte; 76-77 © Kaspars Grinvalds/shutterstock.com; 78 © istockphoto.com/Anthony Baggett; 80 © Rachel Clarke; 83, 85 © istockphoto.com/Duncan Walker; 84 © Jeff Hitchcock; 86 © Roberto Rubio; 87 © Mark William Richardson/shutterstock.com; 91, 92, 104 © ITAR-TASS; 94 LC-USZ62-128730. Courtesy of the Library of Congress Prints and Photographs Division.; 97 © istockphoto.com/Eric Isselée; 99 © Liudmila Gridina/shutterstock.com; 101 Coronation of Tsar Nicholas II (1868-1918) and Tsarina Alexandra Feodorovna (1872-1918) in 1896, 1896 (colour litho), Russian School, (20th century) / Bibliotheque des Arts Decoratifs, Paris, France, Archives Charmet / The Bridgeman Art Library; 103 LC-DIG-ggbain-25191. Courtesy of the Library of Congress Prints and Photographs Division.; 105 LC-USW33-019081-C. Courtesy of the Library of Congress Prints and Photographs Division.; 106 © Sergey Vladimirov, courtesy of Sasha Petite; 108, 117 © Aroo Yamagata; 109, 120 © istockphoto.com/ Peeter Viisimaa; 111 © istockphoto.com/ Hulton Archive; 112 © istockphoto.com/Hulton Archive/Getty Images; 124 © Bob Cheung/shutterstock.com; 125 © istockphoto.com/ kai pak patrick yeung; 127 © istockphoto.com/ Sining Zhang; 128 © Mary Lane/shutterstock.com; 129 © istockphoto.com/ twobluedogs; 131 © istockphoto.com/ Rob Broek; 137 The Emperor Teaon-Kwang Reviewing his Guards, Palace of Peking, from 'China in a Series of Views' by George Newenham Wright (c.1790-1877) 1843 (coloured engraving), Allom, Thomas (1804-72) (after) / Private Collection, The Stapleton Collection / The Bridgeman Art Library; 139 LC-USZ62-97149. Courtesy of the Library of Congress Prints and Photographs Division.; 140 © Bo Pettermann Laugesen

Acknowledgments

MY THANKS TO THE FOLLOWING PEOPLE, who answered my questions, provided information, checked bits of the manuscript, and told me—patiently and courteously—where I had gone wrong:

- Noor al-Saleh of Petra National Trust and Sulieman Farajat of Petra Archaeological Park;
- Diego Manzetti and Viviana Castelli, who shared their knowledge of and love for Rome;
- Linda Martin of Mesa Verde National Park;
- Ann McDougall, who knows Timbuktu, and Rukhsana Khan, who knows Islam;
- John Fudge, student and teacher of English history;
- John McCannon, who answered questions about Russian history and spelling;
- Deborah Sanders, passionate scholar of the Atlantic slave trade; and
- Timothy Brook, who helped with both history and construction details for the Meridian Gate.

Any remaining errors are mine, not theirs.

Thanks are also due to Karen Edwards and David Hik at the University of Alberta, whose assistance made the research for this book possible.

About the author

CLAIRE EAMER WRITES ABOUT science and history and anything else that interests her. As a child, she clambered up the worn steps of a medieval castle in England and touched bullet-scarred walls from the last battle of the Riel Rebellion in Saskatchewan. She has been fascinated by the history in old buildings ever since. Claire has also written *Super Crocs and Monster Wings: Modern Animals' Ancient Past*.